HASHEM/JEHOVAH/YAHWEH:
ALMIGHTY GOD, THE FATHER

BARBARA ANN MARY MACK

© 2021 BARBARA ANN MARY MACK. All rights reserved.

No part of this book may be reproduced, stored in a retrieval system, or transmitted by any means without the written permission of the author.

AuthorHouse™
1663 Liberty Drive
Bloomington, IN 47403
www.authorhouse.com
Phone: 833-262-8899

Because of the dynamic nature of the Internet, any web addresses or links contained in this book may have changed since publication and may no longer be valid. The views expressed in this work are solely those of the author and do not necessarily reflect the views of the publisher, and the publisher hereby disclaims any responsibility for them.

Any people depicted in stock imagery provided by Getty Images are models, and such images are being used for illustrative purposes only.
Certain stock imagery © Getty Images.

This book is printed on acid-free paper.

ISBN: 978-1-6655-4184-8 (sc)
ISBN: 978-1-6655-4183-1 (hc)
ISBN: 978-1-6655-4185-5 (e)

Print information available on the last page.

Published by AuthorHouse 10/26/2021

authorHOUSE

BEHOLD MY PRESENT TESTAMENT: THE CONTINUANCE OF MY OLD AND NEW TESTAMENTS, *SAYS THE LORD JESUS* "VOLUMES SIXTY *AND* SIXTY ONE"

HASHEM/JEHOVAH/YAHWEH: ALMIGHTY GOD, *THE FATHER*
AND
CHRIST *JESUS, OUR REDEEMING GOD*

BY:

BARBARA ANN MARY MACK

BEGAN: AUGUST 27, 2021

COMPLETED: SEPTEMBER 25, 2021

TABLE OF CONTENTS

DEDICATION VII

ACKNOWLEDGMENT VIII

ABOUT THE AUTHOR.. IX

ABOUT THE BOOK X

BOOK ONE 1

BEHOLD MY PRESENT TESTAMENT:
"VOLUME SIXTY" 2

BEHOLD MY PRESENT TESTAMENT:
"VOLUME SIXTY ONE" 100

MY OTHER PUBLISHED BOOKS 143

DEDICATION

TO ALMIGHTY GOD (*HASHEM/JEHOVAH/ YAHWEH/* AND THE OTHER WONDERFUL NAMES THAT GOD, OUR FATHER, IS REFERRED AS) AND MICHAEL AND VANESSA THOMAS, GOD'S BELOVED DAUGHTER AND SON. VANESSA HAS BEEN A DEAR FRIEND OF MINE FOR OVER FORTY YEARS. SHE HAS NEVER FORGOTTEN TO CALL ME ON MY BIRTHDAY EACH YEAR. GOD'S MANY, MANY BLESSINGS TO YOU, DEAR SISTER IN CHRIST *JESUS*

ACKNOWLEDGMENT

OUT OF OBEDIENCE AND LOVE FOR ALMIGHTY GOD, MY DIVINE ORIGIN. I AM A WITNESS TO THE REALITY OF HIS EXISTENCE IN THE MIDST OF US TODAY.

AS HIS HEAVEN SENT PROPHETESS AND MESSENGER, I WILL PROCLAIM AND LIVE HIS HOLY WORDS THAT ARE DICTATED TO ME. HALLELUJAH!!!

BARBARA ANN MARY MACK

ABOUT THE AUTHOR-ALMIGHTY GOD, AND CO-AUTHOR BARBARA ANN MARY MACK

BARBARA ANN MARY MACK IS THE AUTHOR OF FORTY-EIGHT PREVIOUSLY PUBLISHED GOD INSPIRED BOOKS. SHE IS A MISSIONARY MINISTER OF GOD, SERVING HIS CHILDREN OF ALL AGES; SPIRITUALLY AND PHYSICALLY. THROUGH THE YEARS, BARBARA HAS TRAVELED OUTSIDE OF HER COMMUNITY TO MANY LOCATIONS, WHICH INCLUDE ROME, ITALY AND THE WHITE HOUSE; ACCOMPANIED BY HER DAUGHTER, LA TOYA, AND GRANDDAUGHTER, AMYA. WHILE IN COLLEGE, BARBARA'S MAJORS WERE PSYCHOLOGY AND SOCIOLOGY, WITH THE DESIRE TO BECOME A STRESS MANAGEMENT THERAPIST. BUT IN *MARCH OF 1997,* THE LORD GOD BEGAN SPEAKING TO BARBARA AND INSTRUCTING HER TO TAKE DOWN HIS DIVINE MESSAGES AS A SECRETARY TAKES DOWN DICTATIONS FROM HIS OR HER BOSS. *BARBARA HAS WRITTEN OVER SIX THOUSAND* BIBLICAL TYPE BOOKS, OF WHICH THE MAJORITY ARE PUBLISHED WITHIN FIFTY-NINE VOLUMES FORM. BARBARA HAS FIVE CHILDREN'S BOOKS PUBLISHED AT THIS TIME. PRESENTLY, BARBARA RESIDES IN PHILADELPHIA, PENNSYLVANIA.

ABOUT THE BOOK

BOOK ONE: *"HASHEM/JEHOVAH/YAHWEH: ALMIGHTY GOD, THE FATHER"* IS A GOD INSPIRED BOOK THAT CONSISTS OF TWO SEPARATE ADULT BOOKS, WHICH REVEAL *A SPIRITUAL CONVERSATION* BETWEEN ALMIGHTY GOD, THE FATHER, BARBARA ANN MARY MACK, AND GOD'S EARTHLY CHILDREN TODAY.

"HASHEM/JEHOVAH/YAHWEH: ALMIGHTY GOD, THE FATHER" IS WRITTEN IN THE FORM OF *POETRY*, WHICH MAKES IT EASIER FOR THE READER TO FOLLOW AND UNDERSTAND GOD'S WRITTEN SAYINGS THAT FLOW THROUGHOUT THIS BOOK.

"HASHEM/JEHOVAH/YAHWEH: ALMIGHTY GOD, THE FATHER" REVEALS *THE PRESENCE OF GOD, THE FATHER, IN OUR LIVES TODAY.*

BOOK TWO, TITLED: "CHRIST *JESUS, OUR REDEEMING GOD"* REVEALS THE REALITY OF CHRIST *JESUS,* AS OUR REDEEMING GOD AND SAVIOR.

BOOK ONE

GOD'S BLESSED AND BELOVED CHILDREN: KEVIN AND MICHAEL CAMPBELL AND LOVELY SARAH WHEAT. CHILDREN AND FUTURE DAUGHTER IN LAW OF BRENDA CAMPBELL, MY VERY GOOD FRIEND OF OVER FORTY YEARS

BEHOLD MY PRESENT TESTAMENT: THE CONTINUANCE OF MY OLD AND NEW TESTAMENTS, *SAYS THE LORD JESUS* "VOLUME SIXTY"

HASHEM/JEHOVAH/YAHWEH: ALMIGHTY GOD, *THE FATHER*

BY:

BARBARA ANN MARY MACK

BEGAN: AUGUST 27, 2021

COMPLETED: SEPTEMBER 25, 2021

PROLOGUE

I AM HASHEM, ALMIGHTY GOD, THE FATHER

HASHEM, ALMIGHTY GOD, THE FATHER, SPEAKING

I AM HASHEM: ALMIGHTY GOD, THE FATHER.
YOU MAY SEEK A GREATER GOD, BUT THERE IS NO OTHER.

FOR I AM EXISTENCE!!!!
AND I HAVE REVEALED MY HOLY PRESENCE.

I AM JEHOVAH GOD, THE ETERNAL ONE-
I AM THE GOD AND FATHER OF CHRIST JESUS, MY ONLY BEGOTTEN SON.

I HAVE COME, YOU SEE-
FOR I WANT ALL OF MY LOVED ONES TO KNOW OF HOLY ME.

I AM YAHWEH, YOUR LIVING WATERS-
AND I AM REVEALING MY EXISTENCE TO MY CALLED AND SEEKING SONS AND DAUGHTERS.

GET TO KNOW ME, DEAR ONES-
FOR I AM THE CREATOR AND ORIGIN OF MY HEAVENLY AND EARTHLY DAUGHTERS AND SONS.

COME CLOSER TO ME-
SO THAT YOU MAY GET *A SPIRITUAL GLIMPSE OF THE FOREVER-LIVING GOD ALMIGHTY.*

COME CLOSER, DEAR ONE.
FOR I WANT TO *SPEAK TO MY LISTENING DAUGHTER AND SON.*

COME CLOSER TO HASHEM TODAY-
COME CLOSER, SO THAT *YOU MAY HEAR AND LEARN OF EVERYTHING THAT I HAVE TO SAY.*

FOR *I AM ALIVE AND WELL-*
COME CLOSER, SO THAT *YOU MAY UNDERSTAND WHAT I WILL TELL.*

COME CLOSER TO ME TODAY-
SO THAT YOU MAY *HEAR THE HOLY WORDS THAT YOUR GOD AND ORIGIN HAS TO SAY.*

FOR *MY HOLY WORDS OF TRUTH-*
HAVE *GUIDED AND PROTECTED YOU FROM YOUR YOUTH.*

COME, O BLESSED CHILDREN OF MINE!
LISTEN TO *THE HOLY WORDS OF YAHWEH, DURING THIS VERY CRUCIAL PERIOD OF TIME.*

FOR *ALMIGHTY GOD, YOU SEE-*
IS IN THE MIDST OF *THIS WORLD'S TRAGEDY.*

OPEN UP YOUR HEARTS-
LET YOUR HOLY GOD INTO *YOUR REALM OF EXISTENCE BEFORE THE NEXT DAY STARTS.*

FOR *THERE IS NO GUARANTY-*
THAT *YOU WILL FOREVER BE.*

COME TO ME TODAY-
SO THAT I MAY SHARE WITH YOU THE KNOWLEDGE THAT WILL *LEAD YOU TO OUR LIFE SAVING WAY (GOD, THE FATHER, AND CHRIST JESUS, HIS ONLY BEGOTTEN SON).*

FOR *MY ONLY BEGOTTEN SON AND I-*
DO NOT WANT TO *SEE YOUR ETERNAL SOULS DIE.*

COME! COME! COME!

COME, DEAR CHILDREN, AND *ENTER MY EARTHLY KINGDOM!*

FOR *MY KINGDOM ON EARTH-*
EXISTED *BEFORE YOUR PHYSICAL BIRTH.*

COME! COME! COME UNTO ME!
ENTER THE HOLY REALM OF *THE FOREVER EXISTING GOD ALMIGHTY.*

FOR *I DO EXIST!*
I AM PRESENT, DEAR ONES, FOR *I AM WALKING IN YOUR BLESSED MIDST.*

LOOK FOR ME!

LOOK FOR *THE MERCIFUL HASHEM, THE ALMIGHTY!!!*

FOR *HOLY AND TRUE-*
IS *THE GOD AND FATHER WHO SEEKS BELOVED YOU.*

COME, DEAR LITTLE CHILDREN-
FOR *MY REALM IS OPEN TO EVERY PEOPLE AND NATION.*

COME! COME! COME TO ME TODAY!
COME, DEAR CHILDREN, *AS YOU BOW YOUR HEADS TO PRAY.*

FOR *HASHEM, YOUR HEAVENLY GOD AND FATHER, IS NEAR.*
YES! *I AM THE LORD GOD AND FATHER WHO WILL ALWAYS CARE.*

FOR *HOLY, HOLY, HOLY AND TRUE-*
IS *THE LOVE THAT YAHWEH HAS FOR YOU.*

HOLY, HOLY, HOLY AND REAL-
IS *JEHOVAH GOD'S PRESENCE THAT HE WANTS YOU TO FEEL!!!*

FOR *I, JEHOVAH, YOUR FATHER AND GOD-*
DESIRE THAT *YOU ALL RECEIVE A TASTE OF MY EXISTING LOVE.*

FOR *HOLY AND TRUE-*
IS *THE FATHER'S LOVE FOR YOU.*

REMEMBER, DEAR ONES-
REMEMBER *GOD, THE FATHER'S, LOVE, O BLESSED DAUGHTERS AND SONS.*

FOR *HOLY AND TRUE-*
IS *YAHWEH, THE FATHER, LOVE FOR YOU.*

MY REALM OF DIVINITY-
REVEALS THE TRUTH ABOUT *YOUR ORIGIN; GOD ALMIGHTY.*

HOLY, HOLY, HOLY—
IS THE ETERNAL ONE CALLED GOD ALMIGHTY!!!

LET US BEGIN WITH ME, SAYS ALMIGHTY GOD, THE ETERNAL FATHER: YES, I AM SWEET EXISTENCE!!!

THE GATES OF SWEET HEAVEN *HAVE OPENED WIDE*

BARBARA SPEAKING

THE GATES OF SWEET HEAVEN HAVE OPENED WIDE-
AND NOW, *HASHEM/JEHOVAH/YAHWEH;* ALMIGHTY GOD, THE FATHER, *REVEALS A LOVE THAT HE WILL NO LONGER HIDE.*

FOR *HE DID RELEASE-*
HIS ONLY BEGOTTEN SON, *OUR KING OF PEACE.*

FOR *CHRIST JESUS, YOU SEE-*
IS THE REALM OF PEACE THAT *GOD, THE FATHER, HAS GIVEN TO YOU AND ME.*

THE GATES HAVE OPENED WIDE, YOU SEE-
FOR HE HAS *RELEASED THE MIGHTY KING CALLED THE FOREVER-LIVING CHRIST ALMIGHTY.*

HOLY, HOLY, HOLY-
IS *CHRIST JESUS, THE ALMIGHTY!!!*

HE HAS ENTERED THIS EARTH AGAIN-
SO THAT *HE MAY MAKE KNOWN HIS HOLY PRESENCE TO HIS EARTHLY FRIEND* **(THE BELIEVING ONE).**

FOR THOSE WHO *FOLLOW THE TEACHINGS OF CHRIST JESUS-*
WILL *DWELL WITH HIM IN THE LAND OF THE RIGHTEOUS.*

FOR *HOLY AND TRUE-*
IS THE LORD WHO HAS *EXITED THE GATES OF HEAVEN FOR WORTHY ME AND YOU.*

HOLY, HOLY, HOLY-
ARE THE OPENED GATES TO THE HOME OF JEHOVAH GOD, THE ALMIGHTY!!!

FOR HOLY AND TRUE-
ARE THE HEAVENLY GATES THAT ARE OPEN FOR ME AND YOU!!!

O HASHEM: O HOLY GOD AND MIGHTY FATHER

BARBARA SPEAKING TO ALMIGHTY GOD, THE FATHER

O HASHEM: O MIGHTY GOD AND FATHER: O HOLY ONE-
O BLESSED GOD WHO LOVED ME BEFORE AND AFTER THE NEW DAY HAD BEGUN.

O WORTHY ONE ABOVE-
O BLESSED FATHER WHO DESCENDED TO US WITH DIVINE MERCY AND LOVE.

O GREAT ONE-
OH GOD AND FATHER OF THE LIVING CHRIST JESUS, WHO IS YOUR ONLY BEGOTTEN SON.

YOU ARE MAGNIFIED BY YOUR GRACE-
FOR YOU, O HOLY FATHER AND GOD, HAVE NEVER LEFT YOUR NEEDY CHILD'S SMILING FACE.

YOUR MERCY, COMPASSION AND GRACE-
HAVE NEVER ABANDONED THE VULNERABLE HUMAN RACE.

MY GRATEFUL SOUL GIVES YOU CONTINUOUS PRAISE-
AS I COUNT MY BLESSINGS DURING THESE TROUBLED AND TRYING DAYS.

I SALUTE YOU, *O GREAT JEHOVAH, MY GOD AND FATHER!*
I SALUTE YOU! FOR *YOU HAVE NEVER ABANDONED ME, YOUR FAITHFUL MESSENGER AND DAUGHTER.*

OH HOW GRAND-
TO *SIT IN THE PALMS OF YOUR SPIRITUAL LOVING HAND.*

FOR *HOLY AND TRUE-*
ARE *MY LOVE, AND DEVOTION TO YOU.*

FOR YOU, *JEHOVAH, MY EARTHLY AND HEAVENLY LOVE-*
WATCH OVER YOUR BELOVED CHILDREN, *FROM YOUR MIGHTY THRONE IN SWEET HEAVEN ABOVE.*

I WILL FOREVER HONOR YOU, O GREAT AND HOLY *YAHWEH, MY LORD, FATHER AND GOD.*
I WILL ALWAYS *EXPRESS MY FAITHFULNESS AND LOVE.*

FOR YOU HAVE FORMED YOUR CHILDREN *FROM THE DUST OF THAT WAS CALLED INTO EXISTENCE BY HOLY YOU.*

YES! WE WERE FORMED *FROM THE HOLY DUST THAT CAME FROM THE REALM THAT IS CONTINUOUS AND TRUE.*

O HOLY FATHER-
LISTEN TO THE PRAISES THAT *COME FROM THE SPIRIT AND SOUL OF YOUR MESSENGER; BARBARA.*

FOR *I CAN SEE-*
THE HOLY PRESENCE OF *MY GOD AND FATHER, HASHEM, THE ALMIGHTY.*

FOR YOUR HEBREW CHILDREN HAVE BEEN BLESSED WITH KNOWING YOUR HOLY NAME.
YES! HASHEM/JEHOVAH/YAHWEH; ALMIGHTY GOD, THE FATHER, IS THE REALM OF HEAVENLY FAME.

HOLY, HOLY, HOLY-
IS THE GREAT FATHER AND GOD; THE ETERNAL ALMIGHTY!!!

FOR YOU BREATHE; AND EVERYTHING THAT YOU ORDER COMES INTO EXISTENCE.
YOU SPEAK; AND YOUR CREATION IS PERMITTED TO BEHOLD YOUR INFINITE PRESENCE.

FOR HOLY AND TRUE-
ARE THE THINGS THAT ARE FORMED, SPOKEN, AND CREATED BY YOU.

SPEAK, O GREAT ONE, SPEAK!
REVEAL THE HOLY PRESENCE OF MY ORIGIN AND GOD WHOM I LOVE AND SEEK.

SPEAK INTO EXISTENCE-
EVERYTHING THAT WILL GIVE PRAISE, GLORY AND HONOR TO YOUR HOLY PRESENCE.

COME, O SWEET EXISTENCE!
LET HEAVEN AND EARTH WITNESS AND ENJOY YOUR BLESSED AND BELOVED HOLY PRESENCE.

FOR YOUR GREAT CREATION DESIRES TO SEE-
EVERYTHING THAT REVEALS THE ETERNAL FATHER ALMIGHTY.

HOLY, HOLY, HOLY-
IS THE INFINITE REALM OF GOD ALMIGHTY!!!

HASHEM, O GREAT AND HOLY GOD AND FATHER: YOU HAVE COME TO HELP YOUR NEEDY CHILDREN AGAIN

BARBARA SPEAKING TO ALMIGHTY GOD, THE FATHER

O GREAT AND HOLY GOD AND FATHER
YOU HAVE COME BACK TO HELP YOUR NEEDY SON AND DAUGHTER.

YOU ARE OUR STRENGTH, YOU SEE-
AS WE STRUGGLE IN THE PRESENCE OF THE CORONAVIRUS TRAGEDY.

O GREAT AND HOLY HASHEM, OUR HEAVENLY FATHER AND GOD-
I THANK YOU FOR YOUR DIVINE PRESENCE AND LOVE.

FOR WE TRULY NEED, YOU SEE-
THE CONTINUOUS HELP OF GOD, THE ALMIGHTY.

PLEASE HELP US, O GREAT LORD AND GOD.
HELP US WITH YOUR LOVE THAT DESCENDS FROM SWEET HEAVEN ABOVE.

FOR HOLY AND TRUE-
IS MY LOVE FOR ETERNAL YOU.

O GREAT AND BELOVED HASHEM; MY FATHER-
HELP THE LOVED ONES THAT BELONG TO ME, YOUR FAITHFUL MESSENGER AND DAUGHTER.

FOR *HOLY AND TRUE-*
IS OUR LOVE FOR BLESSED YOU.

I BOW IN *THE HOLY PRESENCE OF YOU, MY GOD,*
AS I EXPRESS, EVERY DAY, *MY DEVOTION TO YOU, AND MY LOVE.*

HOLY, HOLY, HOLY-
IS HASHEM, MY GOD AND FATHER ALMIGHTY!!!

IN THE HOLY PRESENCE OF ALMIGHTY GOD (YAHWEH/JEHOVAH/HASHEM)

BARBARA SPEAKING

IN THE HOLY PRESENCE OF *ALMIGHTY GOD, THE FATHER-*
I MOVE WITH *THE HEAVEN SENT WORDS THAT HE DICTATES TO ME, HIS CHOSEN SCRIBE AND DAUGHTER.*

FOR I AM *THE FATHER'S MESSENGER OF DIVINE LOVE-*
HE HAS SENT AND CHOSE ME *TO WRITE DOWN HIS HOLY WORDS THAT DESCEND TO ME FROM SWEET HEAVEN ABOVE.*

FOR *ALMIGHTY GOD, THE FATHER-*
REVEALS HEAVEN'S MYSTERIES TO ME, *HIS CHOSEN SCRIBE AND DAUGHTER.*

FOR *HIS HOLY WORDS, YOU SEE-*
ARE *HEAVENLY MIRACLES THAT ARE GRANTED TO YOU AND ME.*

HOLY, HOLY, HOLY-
ARE *THE HEAVENLY MESSAGES OF YAHWEH, THE ALMIGHTY!!!*

FOR *YAHWEH, YOU SEE-*
IS ONE OF *THE HEBREW NAMES FOR THE ETERNAL FATHER AND ORIGIN OF HUMANITY.*

HOLY IS HIS NAME-
ETERNAL IS HIS FAME!

FOR *HIS GREATNESS, YOU SEE-*
IS RECOGNIZED AND *HONORED BY BLESSED YOU AND ME.*

FOR *YAHWEH, THE GREAT AND HOLY GOD OF THE HEAVENS AND EARTH-*

HAS ASSIGNED ME TO BE *HIS SCRIBE AND MESSENGER BEFORE MY PHYSICAL BIRTH.*

HOLY, HOLY, HOLY-
IS THE GREAT AND ETERNAL *YAHWEH, THE GOD AND FATHER ALMIGHTY!!!*

FOR *HE LIVES, YOU SEE-*
WITHIN THE PHYSICAL PRESENCE OF YOU AND ME.

HOLY, HOLY, HOLY-
IS THE GREAT YAHWEH ALMIGHTY!!!

AND HE *(JEHOVAH/HASHEM/YAHWEH) SPOKE TO ME ONE MORNING*

BARBARA SPEAKING

AND HE, *ALMIGHTY GOD, OUR HEAVENLY FATHER-*
SPOKE TO ME, *HIS BLESSED PROPHETESS AND DAUGHTER.*

HE SPOKE TO ME *EARLY ONE MORNING-*
HE SPOKE ABOUT *THE GOODNESS OF HIS BELOVED SON, CHRIST JESUS, THE HEAVEN SENT KING.*

YES! *YAHWEH, THE HOLY ETERNAL FATHER AND GOD-*
SPOKE TO ME ABOUT *HIS RIVERS OF UNENDING LOVE.*

ALMIGHTY GOD, THE FATHER-
REVEALED TO ME *MANY THINGS THAT HE WANTED TO TELL ME, HIS OBEDIENT DAUGHTER.*

HE TOLD ME THAT *HE TRULY EXIST-*
AND, TODAY, *HE WALKS IN OUR MIDST.*

HE HAS COME TO US-
WITH THE HOLY PRESENCE OF *THE FOREVER-LIVING GOD AND ONLY BEGOTTEN SON, CHRIST JESUS.*

FOR *HASHEM, OUR FATHER AND GOD-*
REVEALS TO ME *THE HEAVENLY SECRETS OF HIS LOVE.*

FOR *HOLY AND TRUE-*
IS HIS LOVE FOR WORTHY ME AND YOU.

AS *JEHOVAH*, ALMIGHTY GOD, THE FATHER, *SITS ON HIS MIGHTY THRONE IN HEAVEN*

JEHOVAH, ALMIGHTY GOD, THE FATHER, SPEAKING

AS I SIT ON MY MIGHTY THRONE IN SWEET HEAVEN-
I LOOK DOWN AT MY CONFUSED, SUFFERING, AND WANDERING CHILDREN.

OH HOW SAD-
TO LOSE THE LOVED ONES THAT I ONCE HAD.

FOR THE CORONAVIRUS, YOU SEE-
DID TAKE SOME WHO DID SERVE HOLY ETERNAL ME.

BUT I WANT MY LOVED ONES TO KNOW FOR SURE-
THAT JESUS, MY ONLY BEGOTTEN SON, WILL ALWAYS BE YOUR SPIRITUAL GUIDE AND MY OPEN DOOR.

FOR, AS I LOOK DOWN FROM MY HEAVENLY THRONE-
I WANT MY EARTHLY LOVED ONES TO KNOW THAT THEY ARE NEVER ALONE.

FOR, OUT OF DIVINE LOVE, YOU SEE-
I DID FORM BLESSED HUMANITY.

FOR HOLY AND TRUE-
IS THE HEAVENLY GOD AND FATHER WHO TRULY LOVES YOU.

AS I SIT-
I WILL RELEASE A LOVE FOR MY CHILDREN THAT WILL NOT QUIT.

FOR *HOLY AND REAL-*
IS MY DIVINE PRESENCE THAT *MY EARTHLY LOVED ONES WILL FEEL.*

FOR *MY LOVE, YOU SEE-*
WILL *ALWAYS SURROUND THE CHILDREN OF JEHOVAH, THE ALMIGHTY.*

WHEN *JEHOVAH* GOD, THE FATHER, *SPEAKS TO HIS EARTHLY* CHILDREN BELOW THE HEAVENS

MARK THORNTON: MY BELOVED SON, SAYS THE LORD GOD

MY BLESSED SON, MARK THORNTON

BARBARA WITH MICHAEL LEONARDO, GOD'S BLESSED AND BELOVED SON

GOD'S MANY BLESSINGS TO ERIC CYRUS, MY NEXT DOOR NEIGHBOR AND ONE OF GOD'S BELOVED SONS. ERIC SHOVELS MY SNOW FOR ME DURING THE WINTER MONTHS, AND I DEEPLY APPRECIATE HIS KINDNESS.

TRAMIER, TIMEEKA, AND THEIR BEAUTIFUL BABY DAUGHTER, A'MIERAH. *GOD'S MANY BLESSINGS TO YOU ALL*

GOD'S MANY BLESSINGS TO MR. CHARLEY JAMES. ENJOY LIFE, DEAR ONE

JEHOVAH, **ALMIGHTY GOD, THE FATHER, SPEAKING**

I SPEAK TO MY CHILDREN EVERY DAY-
FOR *I WANT TO LEAD THEM ALL TO MY HOLY WAY.*

I DO NOT WANT ANY OF THEM TO PERISH, YOU SEE-
I WANT THEM TO LIVE HOLY LIVES FOR ME.

FOR *WITHOUT HOLINESS-*
ONE COULD *NEVER ENTER MY UNENDING REALM OF GOODNESS.*

FOR *HOLY AND TRUE-*
IS THE FATHER WHO PURIFIES YOU.

O HOLY GOD AND FATHER: *MY REJOICING KNEES BEND FOR YOU*

BARBARA SPEAKING TO GOD, THE FATHER

IN YOUR HOLY PRESENCE-
MY REJOICING KNEES BEND FOR YOU, IN MY EARTHLY RESIDENCE.

FOR YOU, O HOLY GOD AND FATHER-
REJOICE ALSO, IN THE PRESENCE OF ME, YOUR FAITHFUL AND OBEDIENT DAUGHTER AND MESSENGER.

FOR MY REJOICING KNEES DO GIVE PRAISE-
TO JEHOVAH GOD, THROUGHOUT THESE QUESTIONABLE DAYS.

MY BLESSED KNEES DO BEND-
IN THE PRESENCE OF ALMIGHTY GOD, MY HEAVENLY FRIEND.

FOR HOLY AND TRUE-
IS THE REJOICING GOD AND FATHER WHO SEES ME THROUGH.

FOR, THROUGH THE ROUGH DAYS-
GOD, OUR HEAVENLY FATHER, ACCEPTS MY SINCERE AND GENEROUS PRAISE.

HOLY, HOLY, HOLY-
ARE THE KNEES THAT BEND IN THE PRESENCE OF THE FATHER ALMIGHTY!!!

FOR HE HAS WITNESSED-
THE INTEGRITY OF MY SERVITUDE AND GOODNESS.

FOR IN HIS HOLY NAME-
I FLEE FROM WORLDLY RECOGNITION AND FAME.

FOR *HOLY AND TRUE-*
ARE *THE GOOD WORKS THAT I DO.*

HOLY, HOLY, HOLY-
ARE MY DAILY WORK FOR GOD ALMIGHTY!!!

BEND, O REJOICING KNEES, BEND!
UNITE WITH *JEHOVAH* GOD, YOUR FATHER, *IN THE MIDST OF THE HEAVENLY ANGELS, CHOIRS, AND ALMIGHTY GOD, YOUR ORIGIN AND FRIEND.*

REJOICE! REJOICE! REJOICE!
GIVE PRAISE, AS YOU *BEND IN THE COMPANY OF THE HEAVENLY CHOIRS UNITED VOICE!*

BEND IN THE MIDST OF HOLINESS-
AS YOU *BEHOLD JEHOVAH GOD'S DIVINE GOODNESS.*

BEND, O BLESSED KNEES; *BEND TODAY-*
BEND, O BLESSED REJOICING KNEES OF MINE, *AS MY EARS LISTEN TO WHAT HE HAS TO SAY.*

FOR HIS HOLY WORDS ARE *REWARDS, YOU SEE-*
THAT ARE *GIVEN TO THE BLESSED CHILDREN OF GOD ALMIGHTY.*

BEND, O BELOVED KNEES THAT *BELONG TO THE DAUGHTER OF JEHOVAH GOD!*
BEND, O BLESSED KNEES OF MINE, *AS YOU BEHOLD HIS REALM OF UNENDING LOVE!!!*

FOR YOU HAVE BEEN CHOSEN, *O BLESSED KNEES OF MINE-*
TO DWELL AND *BEND IN THE HOLY PRESENCE OF ALMIGHTY GOD, THROUGHOUT THE REALM OF UNENDING TIME,*

BEND! BEND! BEND!
BEND, O BLESSED KNEES OF MINE! FOR *YOU HAVE BEEN CHOSEN BY GOD, THE FATHER, YOUR DIVINE ORIGIN AND FRIEND!!!*

JEHOVAH **MY GOD, MY HEAVENLY FATHER:** *I AM LISTENING TO YOU TODAY*

BARBARA SPEAKING TO *JEHOVAH* GOD, THE FATHER

I HEAR YOU SPEAKING TO ME TODAY, DEAR GOD AND FATHER, JEHOVAH.
I WILL RESPOND TO YOUR HOLY WORDS *AS MY SPIRIT RELEASES A HALLELUJAH!*

FOR *YOUR HOLY PRESENCE, YOU SEE-*
BRINGS *GREAT EXCITEMENT TO ME.*

I LISTEN-
TO *EVERY WORDS THAT YOU WANT ME TO SHARE WITH YOUR BLESSED CHILDREN.*

FOR *THEY DO DESIRE-*
THE ONLY WAY (JESUS) TO ESCAPE THE EVERLASTING FIRE.

I AM LISTENING-
TO *THE HOLY GOD AND FATHER OF CHRIST JESUS, OUR SAVIOR AND KING.*

I WILL GO OUT-
WITH A SPIRITUAL SHOUT!

I WILL RELEASE TODAY-
EVERYTHING THAT GOD, THE FATHER, HAS TO SAY.

FOR HOLY AND TRUE-
IS THE MESSENGER (BARBARA) WHO IS SENT BY HOLY YOU.

SPEAK, O HOLY ONE-
REVEAL THE HOLY WORDS THAT YOU WANT ME TO SHARE
WITH YOUR BLESSED DAUGHTER AND SON.

FOR I DO LISTEN-
TO THE HOLY VOICE WHO SPEAKS TO EVERY NATION.

HOLY, HOLY, HOLY-
IS THE GOD AND FATHER ALMIGHTY!!!

MY FATHER: MY ORIGIN: MY DIVINE CONNECTION: ALMIGHTY GOD JEHOVAH

BARBARA SPEAKING TO ALMIGHTY GOD JEHOVAH

O HOLY JEHOVAH, MY DIVINE ORIGIN-
MY HOLY GOD, AND MY ETERNAL FRIEND.

YOU, O HOLY AND GREAT ONE-
ARE THE ORIGIN OF JESUS, YOUR ONLY BEGOTTEN SON.

GOD OF LOVE, AND MY REDEEMING REALM OF HOPE-
THE HOLY GOD WHO HELPS HIS EARTHLY LOVED ONES COPE.

O HOLY JEHOVAH, OUR LIVING LORD, GOD AND KING-
YOU ARE CREATOR OF EVERY GOOD THING.

YOU ARE THE FATHER OF DIVINE LOVE-
THAT COMES TO YOUR NEEDY CHILDREN TODAY, IN THE FORM OF A FREE FLYING DOVE.

YOUR REALM OF HOLINESS-
REVEALS YOUR CONTINUOUS MERCY AND GOODNESS.

O HOLY ONE-
THROUGHOUT EVERY DAY, YOU CALL YOUR CHOSEN DAUGHTER AND SON.

YOU CALL AND GUIDE US INTO YOUR REALM OF THE RIGHTEOUS-
SO THAT WE MAY IMITATE AND WITNESS THE OBEDIENCE AND FAITHFULNESS OF THE FOREVER-LIVING GOD AND LORD CHRIST JESUS.

O HOLY GOD AND FATHER ABOVE-
I THANK YOU FOR SHARING YOUR BELOVED SON, CHRIST JESUS, YOUR GREATEST EXPRESSION OF CONTINUOUS DIVINE LOVE.

HOLY, HOLY, HOLY-
IS THE GREAT AND ONLY JEHOVAH, THE ALMIGHTY!!!

HALLELUJAH! HALLELUJAH! HALLELUJAH- TO OUR MIGHTY GOD AND FATHER, JEHOVAH!!!

BARBARA SPEAKING

GIVE HIM PRAISE! GIVE HIM PRAISE!
GIVE ALMIGHTY GOD, THE FATHER, PRAISE, THROUGHOUT THESE PANDEMIC DAYS!

SING HALLELUJAH-
TO OUR GREAT GOD, O HOLY JEHOVAH!

HE HAS SET US FREE-
FOR, WE ARE THE LOVED ONES OF GOD, THE FATHER; THE ALMIGHTY.

HE HAS SET US FREE-
FROM THE CLUTCHES OF SIN THAT HAD CAPTURED YOU AND ME.

BUT GOD, OUR HEAVENLY FATHER-
HAS COME TO RELEASE HIS EARTHLY SON AND DAUGHTER.

GIVE HIM PRAISE, O BLESSED ONE!
GIVE PRAISE TO THE GOD AND FATHER OF THE FAITHFUL AND OBEDIENT DAUGHTER AND SON.

FOR HE RULES, YOU SEE-
OVER THE REALM THAT CALLS YOU AND ME.

HOLY, HOLY, HOLY-
IS JEHOVAH GOD, ALMIGHTY!!!

JEHOVAH GOD, MY FATHER

BARBARA SPEAKING TO ALMIGHTY GOD JEHOVAH

YOU SPEAK, AND YOUR HOLY WORD IS EXISTENCE.
YOU HAVE SPOKEN TO ME IN THE MIDST OF MY EARTHLY HUMBLE RESIDENCE.

YOUR WORD IS FINALITY-
BECAUSE YOU ARE THE FOREVER LIVING GOD ALMIGHTY.

YOU, O GREAT AND HOLY FATHER-
HAVE BROUGHT INTO EXISTENCE THE THINGS THAT GIVE COMFORT TO ME, YOUR OBEDIENT MESSENGER AND DAUGHTER.

I GIVE YOU CONTINUOUS PRAISE-
DURING THESE PANDEMIC DAYS.

FOR HOLY AND TRUE.
ARE THE WORDS AND MANIFESTATIONS THAT COME FROM YOU.

HOLY, HOLY, HOLY-
IS JEHOVAH GOD, THE ALMIGHTY!!!

WHEN MY SPIRIT AND SOUL *BOW IN THE HOLY PRESENCE OF ALMIGHTY GOD, YAHWEH*

BARBARA SPEAKING

I BOW IN THE HOLY PRESENCE OF *YAHWEH, GOD, THE FATHER-*
AS I EXPRESS THE LOVE AND DEVOTION OF *HIS FAITHFUL MESSENGER AND HEAVEN SENT DAUGHTER.*

MY *TOTAL BEING-*
REJOICES IN THE PRESENCE OF *THE HOLY GOD AND FATHER WHO CREATED EVERY GOOD AND PROFITABLE THING.*

MY BODY AND SOUL *LEAP WITH GRATITUDE-*
AS I DANCE IN THE MIDST OF *THE HEAVENLY MULTITUDE.*

O WHAT A JOY IT IS TODAY-
TO BE IN *THE HOLY PRESENCE OF ALMIGHTY GOD, THE ETERNAL YAHWEH.*

HOLY, HOLY, HOLY-
IS THE GOD AND FATHER; THE ALMIGHTY!!!

FOR *YAHWEH, MY HOLY SPIRITUAL AND PHYSICAL GUIDE-*
REVEALS TO ME *A DIVINE LOVE THAT I WILL NOT HIDE.*

FOR *WHEN HE SPEAKS TO ME-*
I HOLD ON TO THE HOLY SPIRIT THAT IS RELEASED BY *GOD, THE ALMIGHTY.*

FOR *HOLY AND TRUE-*
IS *THE FATHER WHO SPEAKS TO ME AND YOU.*

HOLY, HOLY, HOLY-
IS THE FOREVER REIGNING YAHWEH ALMIGHTY!!!

FOR *HE SITS ON HIS MIGHTY THRONE ON HIGH-*
AS HE RELEASES HIS GOOD NEWS THAT *HIS BELIEVING CHILDREN WILL NOT ABANDON NOR DENY.*

HOLY, HOLY, HOLY-
IS THE GOOD NEWS OF THE FATHER ALMIGHTY!!!

YAHWEH, THE GREAT AND HOLY GOD AND FATHER OF THE HEBREWS *IS IN OUR MIDST TODAY*

BARBARA SPEAKING

Yahweh, the great and holy God and Father of the Hebrews is in our midst today, dear ones.
His holy presence is welcomed by his suffering and believing daughters and sons.

He walks in the midst of all of us-
as we take cover from the devastation and destruction of the coronavirus.

He sees everything, you see-
and the believing ones will receive needed help and guidance from Yahweh, the Almighty.

For his holy presence, you see-
moves within sent and obedient me.

BARBARA SPEAKING TO GOD, THE FATHER, YAHWEH

Move within me, O precious and beloved God and Father.
Move within the purified being of me, your obedient messenger and daughter.

For holy, holy, holy-
is the eternal God and Father, Yahweh, the Almighty!!!

I will follow your holy spirit and presence that moves within me.
I will follow the holy presence of Yahweh, the Almighty!!!

FOR WITHIN ME-
DWELLS THE FOREVER-LIVING ALMIGHTY.

HOLY, HOLY, HOLY-
IS THE PRESENCE OF GOD ALMIGHTY!!!

HIS HOLY SPIRIT MOVES, YOU SEE-
IN THE MIDST OF HIS CHILDREN AND ME.

HE MOVES WITH HIS GREAT CREATION-
AS HE WHISPERS TO EVERY PEOPLE AND NATION.

HOLY, HOLY, HOLY-
IS THE FOREVER-LIVING YAHWEH ALMIGHTY!!!

O LORD MY GOD: MY FATHER

BARBARA SPEAKING TO ALMIGHTY GOD, THE FATHER

O LORD, MY GOD-
O GRACIOUS FATHER ALMIGHTY, WHOM I WILL ALWAYS LOVE.

YOU SPEAK TO YOUR BELOVED CHILDREN-
FROM EVERY PEOPLE, LAND AND NATION.

YOUR REALM OF HOLINESS AND LOVE-
REVEALS YOUR GOODNESS AND EXISTENCE IN SWEET HEAVEN ABOVE.

YOUR DIVINITY-
REVEALS YOUR UNENDING REALITY.

YOU, O HOLY GOD AND FATHER, DO EXIST.
FOR YOUR BLESSED HOLY SPIRIT MOVES WITHIN OUR MIDST.

BARBARA SPEAKING TO EARTH'S INHABITANTS

HOLY, HOLY, HOLY-
IS THE VISIBLE SPIRIT AND PRESENCE OF GOD, THE FATHER ALMIGHTY.

FOR *HE REALLY DOES EXIST-*
IN OUR BLESSED MIDST.

BEHOLD! BEHOLD! BEHOLD!
LOOK UPON HIS HOLY WORD OF OLD!!!

FOR *HE HAS SPOKEN-*
TO HIS NEEDY AND WELL-LOVED VULNERABLE CHILDREN.

BEHOLD *THE HOLY PRESENCE OF ALMIGHTY GOD, TODAY-*
AS *HE REVEALS HIS LIFE REWARDING HOLY WAY.*

FOR HIS WAY IS *HOLY AND PURE, YOU SEE-*
HIS WAY INVITES THE SINLESS ONES TO THE REALM THAT RELEASES *HIS GLORY AND DIVINITY.*

HOLY, HOLY, HOLY-
IS THE ONLY WAY TO THE HEAVENLY HOME OF GOD ALMIGHTY!!!

ALMIGHTY GOD AND HIS BELOVED CHILDREN

Such a beautiful couple of the Jewish faith. We met at a hotel during my missionary work for the Lord God in New Hampshire. They were very interested in my calling and ministry.

MET THESE GENTLEMEN AT CONNECTICUT'S STATE CAPITOL BUILDING DURING MY MISSIONARY WORK FOR THE LORD GOD IN CONNECTICUT

MET THESE WONDERFUL PEOPLE FROM PARIS, FRANCE, DURING OUR MISSIONARY WORK FOR THE LORD GOD IN AUGUST OF 2016. WE STILL COMMUNICATE VIA FACEBOOK IN 2021

ARCHBISHOP OF ANGLICAN DIOCESE OF KUMASI, MOST REVEREND PROFESSOR DANIEL YINKAH SARFO, AND PROPHETESS BARBARA ANN MARY MACK, AT A CHURCH IN PHILADELPHIA, PA

MET THIS WONDERFUL DOCTOR AND HIS LOVELY FAM AT A HOTEL WE WERE STAYING AT IN NEW HAMPSHIRE. HE TOLD US THAT HE LOVES THE LORD GOD

MET THIS BLESSED COUPLE IN ORLANDO, FLORIDA, DURING OUR MISSIONARY WORK FOR THE LORD GOD. THEY ARE BELIEVERS IN THE FOREVER-LIVING CHRIST *JESUS*

THESE WONDERFUL SEMINARIANS AND FR. CARLOS VISITED OUR HOME DURING THEIR DOOR TO DOOR MINISTRY IN OUR NEIGHBORHOOD.

MET THIS WONDERFUL HUSBAND AND WIFE AT THEIR BED AND BREAKFAST PLACE IN NORTHEAST PENNSLYVANIA DURING MY MISSIONARY WORK FOR THE LORD GOD. THEY PURCHASED ONE OF MY GOD INSPIRED BOOKS BEFORE WE LEFT THEIR ESTABLISHMENT.

BARBARA WITH A WONDERFUL GOD FEARING PRIEST FROM INDIA

BARBARA WITH FAYE: A COLLEGE STUDENT INTERVIEWING ME, AS I PRAYED IN FRONT OF THE WHITE HOUSE

FATHER KEN BRABAZON, MY SPIRITUAL SON IN THE LIVING CHRIST *JESUS*. MY FAM AND I HAVE KNOWN FR. KEN SINCE HE WAS IN HIGH SCHOOL. I WAS VERY PROUD TO ATTEND HIS ORDINATION INTO THE PRIESTHOOD. GOD'S MANY BLESSINGS TO THIS YOUNG MAN, A TRUE SON OF GOD

LA TOYA WITH OUR TWO HANDSOME COUSINS, KIETH AND CHRIS WILLIAMS

MY BEAUTIFUL AUNT RAYE: MY MOTHER'S ELDEST SISTER

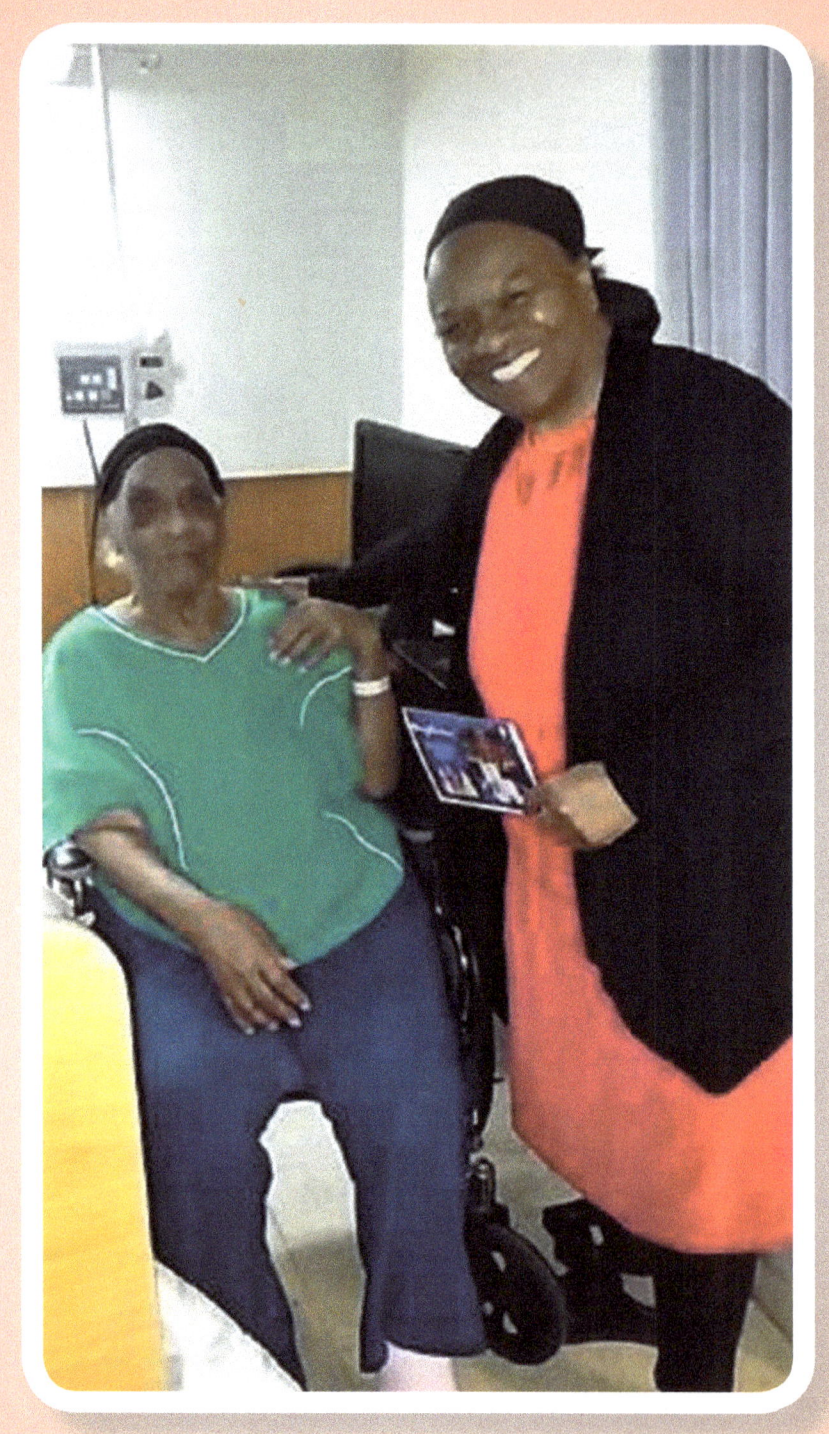

FR. MARIANO: PASTOR OF SAINT BARNABAS CHURCH. HE TOO, READ MY GOD INSPIRED BOOKS. A WONDERFUL PASTOR. GOD'S MANY BLESSINGS TO FR. MARIANO

WE MET THESE FINE OFFICERS DURING OUR MISSIONARY WORK FOR THE LORD GOD IN DOWNTOWN NEW YORK, IN AUGUST OF 2016. WE TALKED ABOUT MY WORK FOR THE LORD FOR NEARLY AN HOUR. WE HAD A GREAT TIME AND CONVERSATION

WE MET THESE BLESSED SECURITY OFFICERS AFTER TOURING THE 911 SITE IN LOWER MANHATTAN, NEW YORK, IN AUGUST OF 2016

WE MET THIS WONDERFUL GENTLEMAN, NELSON, AT THE LOMBARDY HOTEL DURING OUR MISSIONARY WORK FOR THE LORD GOD IN DOWNTOWN MANHATTAN, NEW YORK, IN AUGUST OF 2016

WE MET THIS GOD FEARING YOUNG MAN AT HIS ICE CREAM STAND IN TIMES SQUARE, NEW YORK, DURING OUR MISSIONARY WORK FOR THE LORD GOD IN AUGUST OF 2016

WE MET THESE THREE BLESSED GENTLEMEN DURING OUR MISSIONARY WORK FOR THE LORD GOD IN CONNECTICUT, IN 2016

WE MET THIS GENTLEMAN (ALBERTUS) AT A PARK IN CONNECTICUT, DURING OUR MISSIONARY WORK FOR THE LORD GOD IN 2016/ GOD'S MANY BLESSINGS TO HIS SON, ALBERTUS

WE MET THIS BEAUTIFUL REPORTER (SUE) AT THE STATE'S CAPITOL BUILDING IN CONNECTICUT, IN 2016. SHE WAS VERY KIND AND FRIENDLY. GOD'S MANY BLESSINGS TO SUE

MET THIS BLESSED GENTLEMAN (JOHN) AT HIS SOUVENIR SHOP IN BOSTON, MASSACHUSETTS, DURING OUR MISSIONARY WORK FOR THE LORD GOD

BEAUTIFUL AND BLESSED BARBARA, WHOM WE MET DURING OUR MISSIONARY WORK FOR THE LORD GOD IN 2016

MET THESE GENTLEMEN AT RHODE ISLAND'S STATE CAPITOL BUILDING DURING OUR MISSIONARY WORK FOR THE LORD GOD IN 2016

HAVING A WONDERFUL AND BLESSED CONVERSATION WITH THE CLERGY AT A CHURCH IN PHILADELPHIA, PA, DURING MY MISSIONARY WORK FOR THE LORD GOD

ALMIGHTY GOD SPEAKING TO EARTH'S INHABITANTS TODAY

My children! My children! My children!
Yes! I am speaking to my loved ones from every nation.

I am speaking to *those whom my Holy Spirit does love.*
I am speaking to you *from my mighty throne above.*

Receive my gift of love-
That descended with *my only begotten Son (Christ Jesus) from heaven above.*

Receive *my gift of life-*
That is *granted to every blessed husband and wife.*

For *my gift, you see-*
Reveals a taste of *the forever-living me.*

Receive me, dear ones.
Receive your heavenly Father, *O beloved daughters and sons.*

For *holy, you see-*
Is *the God who loves the children who believe in eternal me.*

Holy, holy, holy-
Is the eternal Father Almighty!!!

Yahweh: My Lord *and my God*

BARBARA SPEAKING TO ALMIGHTY GOD, THE FATHER

O HOLY FATHER ABOVE-
I THANK YOU FOR SENDING TO YOUR EARTHLY CHILDREN,
YOUR REALM OF DIVINE LOVE.

O HOLY YAHWEH, MY HEAVENLY GOD AND FATHER-
I PRAISE YOU FOR TRUSTING ME, YOUR OBEDIENT MESSENGER AND DAUGHTER.

FOR YOU TRUST ME WITH THE DELIVERANCE OF YOUR HOLY WORDS OF LOVE-
THAT YOU SEND TO ME FROM YOUR HEAVENLY THRONE ABOVE.

OH HOW GRAND-
OH WHAT A DELIGHT-
TO HAVE YOUR HOLY SPIRIT AND PRESENCE WITHIN MY HUMBLED SIGHT.

FOR YOUR REALM OF HOLINESS AND MERCY-
HAS HUMBLED BELOVED AND BLESSED ME.

O GREAT AND HOLY ONE-
I THANK YOU FOR TRUSTING ME WITH THE SOULS OF YOUR CALLED AND CHOSEN DAUGHTER AND SON.

HOLY, HOLY, HOLY-
IS THE LOVE OF YAHWEH, THE ALMIGHTY!!!

YOU ARE THE REALM OF GOODNESS-
YOUR PRESENCE ALONE, REVEALS YOUR COMPASSION AND HOLINESS.

I BOW! I BOW! *I BOW EVERY DAY-*
AS *I LISTEN TO YAHWEH'S HOLY, HOLY WAY.*

HALLELUJAH! HALLELUJAH! HALLELUJAH IS THE PRAISE-
THAT MY BLESSED SOUL SINGS THROUGHOUT THESE PANDEMIC DAYS!!!
I WILL WALK WITH *YAHWEH; GOD, THE FATHER, TODAY*

BARBARA SPEAKING TO *YAHWEH*, ALMIGHTY GOD, THE FATHER

HOLD MY HAND TIGHT, DEAR *YAHWEH, MY HEAVENLY GOD AND FATHER.*
HOLD TIGHT, *YOUR OBEDIENT MESSENGER AND DAUGHTER.*

FOR SATAN'S *REALM OF EVIL, YOU SEE-*
TRIES TO HINDER OBEDIENT ME.

HE TRIES, *YOU SEE-*
TO PREVENT ME FROM *SHARING THE HEAVENLY MESSAGES THAT COME FROM BLESSED THEE.*

BUT HE WILL *NEVER PREVENT ME, YOU SEE-*
FOR I KNOW THAT *YAHWEH, MY HEAVENLY GOD AND FATHER, IS HOLDING ON VERY TIGHT TO VULNERABLE ME.*

HOLY, HOLY, HOLY-
ARE THE LOVING SURROUNDING ARMS OF GOD, THE FATHER, ALMIGHTY!!!

AS I WALK WITH *YAHWEH, THE FATHER, TODAY-*
I WILL *LEAD HIS CALLED ONES TO HIS LIFE REWARDING HOLY WAY.*

FOR THROUGH *HIS ONLY BEGOTTEN SON, CHRIST JESUS-*
HE SAVES ALL OF US.

FOR OUR OBEDIENCE UNTO *JESUS' ONLY GOD AND FATHER-*
WILL ALLOW US TO BE CALLED *HIS BELOVED AND BLESSED SON AND DAUGHTER.*

FOR *HOLY AND TRUE-*
IS THE GOD AND FATHER WHO *WATCHES OVER ME AND YOU.*

HOLY, HOLY, HOLY-
IS YAHWEH; GOD ALMIGHTY!!!

AND HE, *YAHWEH, GOD, THE FATHER, SUMMONED ME*

<u>*YAHWEH;*</u> **GOD, THE FATHER, SPEAKING TO BARBARA, HIS PROPHETESS AND MESSENGER**

COME! COME! COME, O BLESSED DAUGHTER OF MINE!
FOR I NEED YOU TO *SHARE MY HOLY MESSAGES WITH MY LOVED ONES DURING THIS PANDEMIC PERIOD OF TIME.*

I NEED YOU TO RELEASE-
THE GOOD NEWS THAT *REVEAL MY HEAVENLY REALM OF PEACE.*

FOR *I WANT MY LOVED ONES TO KNOW-*
THAT *I AM WITH YOU ALL WHEREVER YOU GO.*

DO NOT BE AFRAID, DEAR ONES-
FOR THE CORONAVIRUS CAN NEVER DESTROY *MY FAITHFUL DAUGHTERS AND SONS.*

GO, DEAR BARBARA!
DELIVER MY WORDS OF COMFORT AND PEACE *TO MY SUFFERING SON AND DAUGHTER.*

LET THEM KNOW FOR ME-
THAT *I AM THE CONQUERING GOD ALMIGHTY!!!*

FOR WHEN *I, THE FOREVER LIVING YAHWEH, THE FATHER, SPEAKS-*
MY VOICE IS HEARD BY *THE BLESSED SOULS WHOM I DO SEEK.*

SO, *GO! GO! GO, DEAR BARBARA!*
REVEAL MY HOLY PRESENCE TO *MY HURTING CHILDREN, DEAR DAUGHTER.*

GO TO THEM TODAY!
SPEAK THE WORDS THAT *I, YOUR HEAVENLY GOD AND FATHER, YAHWEH, COMMANDS YOU TO SAY!*

FOR *HOLY AND TRUE-*
ARE THE WORDS THAT *I SPEAK THROUGH BLESSED YOU.*

AS I LOOK UP TOWARDS *SWEET HEAVEN ABOVE*

BARBARA SPEAKING

AS *I LOOK UP TOWARDS SWEET HEAVEN ABOVE-*
I BEHOLD *THE BEAUTY AND MAGNIFICENCE OF JEHOVAH GOD, THE FATHER'S, REALM OF LOVE.*

FOR *I CAN BEHOLD AND FEEL-*
A DIVINE LOVE AND PRESENCE THAT ARE *ETERNAL AND REAL.*

AS *I LOOK-*
HE, ALMIGHTY GOD, *JEHOVAH, GIVES ME THE HOLY WORDS THAT HE WANTS ME TO INCLUDE IN MY HEAVENLY DICTATED BOOK.*

FOR *JEHOVAH GOD, THE FATHER, YOU SEE-*
DICTATES HIS HOLY WORDS TO ME.

AS *I LOOK UP TOWARD HEAVEN WITH GREAT JOY-*
I RECEIVE THE FATHER'S MESSAGES THAT *HE HAS FOR HIS BELOVED LITTLE GIRL AND BOY.*

FOR *ALMIGHTY GOD, THE FATHER-*
TRUSTS ME, *HIS HEAVEN SENT DAUGHTER.*

HOLY, HOLY, HOLY-
IS ALMIGHTY GOD'S MESSENGER (BARBARA), WHO IS TRUST WORTHY!!!

FOR *OUT OF OBEDIENCE, YOU SEE-*
I RECEIVE THE HOLY WORDS THAT *COME FROM THE FOREVER-LIVING BEING OF THE FATHER ALMIGHTY.*

HOLY, HOLY, HOLY-
IS JEHOVAH GOD, THE ALMIGHTY!!!

AS ALMIGHTY GOD *JEHOVAH, LEADS ME TO HIS CHOSEN NATION*

BARBARA SPEAKING

AS JEHOVAH GOD, THE FATHER, LEADS ME TO HIS CHOSEN NATION-
I WILL SPEAK THE HOLY WORDS THAT ARE REVEALED TO ME FOR HIS BLESSED CHILDREN.

AS HE LEADS ME TO HIS BLESSED NATION-
I WILL BOW UNTO HIM WITH HIS BELIEVING CHILDREN.

FOR HOLY AND TRUE-
IS THE GOD AND FATHER WHO CREATED ME AND YOU.

AS JEHOVAH GOD LEADS ME-
I WILL SHARE HIS MESSAGES OF LOVE WITH THE OFFSPRING OF GOD ALMIGHTY.

FOR HOLY AND REAL-
IS THE HEAVENLY PRESENCE THAT I CAN TRULY FEEL.

HOLY, HOLY, HOLY-

IS MY GOD AND FATHER, JEHOVAH, THE ALMIGHTY!!!

ALMIGHTY GOD, HAS GIVEN ME STEWARDSHIP, SAYS BARBARA ANN MARY MACK

ALMIGHTY GOD, THE FATHER, SPEAKING TO BARBARA, HIS SENT MESSENGER

I, JEHOVAH, YOUR GOD-
HAVE GIVEN YOU, DEAR BARBARA, STEWARDSHIP OVER MY FLOCK OF LOVE.

FOR *I DO-*
TRUST *HOLY AND SENT YOU.*

I HAVE GIVEN YOU *STEWARDSHIP, YOU SEE-*
OVER THE LOVED ONES WHO ARE *CALLED AND CHOSEN BY ME.*

I HAVE GIVEN YOU *STEWARDSHIP OVER YOUR BLESSED DAUGHTER AND GRANDDAUGHTER-*
FOR I HAVE SENT MY QUEEN OF HEAVEN, YES! *MY LOVELY DAUGHTER AND MESSENGER; BARBARA.*

FOR *YOU ARE THEIR HEAVEN SENT GUIDE-*
YOU ARE *COMMISSIONED BY GOD, YOUR FATHER, TO EXHIBIT A DIVINE LOVE THAT I WILL NOT HIDE.*

YOU, DEAR BARBARA:

I HAVE GIVEN STEWARDSHIP OVER LA TOYA AND AMYA, YOUR BLESSED AND BELOVED DAUGHTER AND GRANDDAUGHTER.

EXHIBIT ME, DEAR BARBARA!
EXHIBIT THE LOVE, COMPASSION, AND MERCY OF *JEHOVAH GOD, YOUR HEAVENLY ORIGIN AND FATHER.*

FOR *HOLY AND TRUE-*
IS THE TRUST THAT I HAVE PLACED IN YOU.

WHEN ALMIGHTY GOD, THE FATHER, *SPEAKS TO ME*

BARBARA SPEAKING

WHEN *ALMIGHTY GOD, THE FATHER, SPEAKS TO ME-*

MY BLESSED SPIRIT AND SOUL *UNITE WITH CHRIST JESUS, HIS ONLY BEGOTTEN SON; THE ALMIGHTY.*

HE IS *THE ONLY BEGOTTEN SON OF GOD, THE FATHER-* AND *HE IS MY LORD, GOD, AND SAVIOR.*

MY BLESSED *SOUL DOES REJOICE-* AS MY TOTAL BEING IS *CAPTURED BY HIS HOLY VOICE.*

FOR, *ALMIGHTY GOD, THE FOREVER-LIVING FATHER-* SPEAKS DAILY, TO ME, *HIS OBEDIENT AND DEVOTED DAUGHTER.*

FOR *MY OBEDIENT BEING-* LISTENS EVERY MOMENT OF THE DAY, FOR *THE VOICE OF ALMIGHTY GOD, THE ETERNAL KING.*

FOR *HOLY AND TRUE-* ARE THE WORDS THAT *ALMIGHTY GOD REVEALS TO ME AND YOU.*

I DO LISTEN EVERY DAY- TO MY HOLY FATHER AND GOD, *AS I LEAD HIS CHILDREN TO HIS RIGHTEOUS AND HOLY WAY.*

HOLY, HOLY, HOLY- *IS GOD, THE ALMIGHTY!!!*

FOR *HE DOES REIGN, YOU SEE-* *IN THE MIDST OF YOU AND ME!!!*

WAKE UP! WAKE UP! FOR *ALMIGHTY GOD, THE FATHER, IS IN OUR MIDST*

ALMIGHTY GOD, THE FATHER, SPEAKING

I AM IN YOUR BLESSED MIDST, DEAR CHILDREN.
I AM IN THE MIDST OF EVERY NATION.

I CAN SEE-
EVERYTHING THAT BELONGS TO ME.

I CAN SEE YOUR PAIN AND SORROW-
I CAN SEE YOUR DESPAIR, AS YOU HOPE FOR A BETTER TOMORROW.

I CAN SEE-
THE WEARY CHILDREN WHO BELONG TO ME.

I WILL RESCUE-
ALL OF YOU!!!

LISTEN AND FOLLOW-
IF YOU DESIRE A LIFE REWARDING TOMORROW.

FOR ONLY I CAN-
BRING RELIEF TO EVERY SUFFERING WOMAN AND MAN.

FOR I AM JEHOVAH GOD, YOUR HEAVENLY CREATOR-
I AM YOUR ETERNAL GOD AND FATHER!!!

WALK TOWARDS ME, YOUR ONLY HOPE, SAYS ALMIGHTY GOD, THE FOREVER-LIVING FATHER

ALMIGHTY GOD, THE FATHER, SPEAKING

DEAR CHILDREN-
YES! YOU FROM EVERY NATION.

WALK TOWARDS *MY REALM OF HOLINESS-*
SO THAT YOU MAY *EXPERIENCE MY LIFE TIME OF GOODNESS.*

WALK TOWARDS *YOUR HEAVENLY GOD AND FATHER-*
AS *I SPEAK THE WORDS THAT WILL HELP AND GUIDE MY NEEDY SON AND DAUGHTER.*

WALK TOWARDS ME-
WALK IN THE DIRECTION THAT WILL *LEAD YOU TO MY KINGDOM AND GLORY.*

FOLLOW MY ONLY WAY-
AS YOU *TRAVEL THROUGHOUT YOUR DAY.*

FOR *I WILL HELP, YOU SEE-*
THOSE WHO WALK WITH ETERNAL ME.

I CAN SEE

<u>*HASHEM*</u>**, ALMIGHTY GOD, THE FATHER, SPEAKING**

I *HASHEM, YOUR ALMIGHTY GOD AND FATHER-*
DO SEE EVERYTHING THAT *INVOLVES MY EARTHLY SON AND DAUGHTER.*

FOR, *AS YOUR DIVINE CREATOR-*
I WILL *BRING PEACE TO MY FAITHFUL AND OBEDIENT SON AND DAUGHTER.*

FOR, *THE CORONAVIRUS-*
CAN *NEVER DESTROY THE ETERNAL SOULS OF THE RIGHTEOUS.*

MY CHILDREN: *LIVE RIGHT-*
FOR *HASHEM,* YOUR HEAVENLY GOD AND FATHER, *ALWAYS HAS YOU IN HIS SIGHT.*

DO NOT THINK THAT I-
ONLY EXIST ABOVE THE SKY.

FOR *I CAN SEE-*
EVERYTHING THAT WAS *FORMED AND CREATED BY ETERNAL ME.*

FOR *HOLY AND TRUE-*
IS THE ONE WHO CREATED YOU.

I CAN SEE IT ALL-
I CAN FEEL AND SEE *THOSE WHO HAVE ANSWERED AND HONORED MY HOLY CALL.*

FOR *I HAVE CALLED MANY-*
TO *SHARE THE THRONE OF HASHEM; GOD, THE FATHER ALMIGHTY.*

COME, DEAR CHILDREN!
FOR *HASHEM,* YOUR HEAVENLY GOD AND FATHER, *LOVES HIS GREATEST CREATION.*

COME! COME! COME!
ENTER HASHEM'S HOLY KINGDOM!!!

FOR *MY HOLY KINGDOM, YOU SEE-*
IS AN *EVERLASTING KINGDOM THAT IS RULED AND REIGNED BY GOD, THE ALMIGHTY.*

HOLY, HOLY, HOLY-
IS THE KINGDOM OF HASHEM, THE FATHER ALMIGHTY!!!

ALMIGHTY GOD, THE ETERNAL FATHER, IS SEATED ON HIS HEAVENLY THRONE

ALMIGHTY GOD, THE FATHER, SPEAKING

FROM MY HOLY THRONE OF LOVE-
I SEND DOWN DIVINE MESSAGES FROM SWEET HEAVEN ABOVE.

MY DESCENDED MESSAGES, YOU SEE-
ARE FOR *THE LOVED ONES WHO ARE CALLED AND CHOSEN BY ME.*

ALMIGHTY GOD, THE FATHER, SPEAKING

RECEIVE MY HOLY WORDS, *O BLESSED DAUGHTER OF MINE.*
FOR THIS IS *A VERY CRUCIAL AND DANGEROUS PERIOD OF TIME.*

RECEIVE *MY HOLY MESSAGES OF SALVATION-*
THAT ARE *GRANTED TO EVERY PEOPLE AND NATION.*

RECEIVE *MY HOLY MESSAGES OF LOVE, DEAR DAUGHTER.*
RECEIVE THE LIFE SAVING WORDS THAT COME FROM *JEHOVAH GOD, YOUR HEAVENLY ORIGIN AND FATHER.*

FOR *HOLY AND TRUE-*
ARE THE MESSAGES THAT ARE GIVEN TO YOU.

HOLY, HOLY, HOLY-
ARE THE MESSAGES OF GOD ALMIGHTY!!!

When the voice of Jehovah God speaks from His mighty throne

<u>Jehovah God, the Father, speaking to Barbara, His sent messenger and scribe</u>

Listen to My holy voice, dear daughter of Mine-
For I want you to speak to My loved ones during this devastating period of time.

Tell them for Me-
That they must follow the teachings of My beloved only begotten Son, Christ Almighty.

For I have given unto He-
Divine authority.

He has authority, you see-
To lead Our children to the realm of sweet eternity.

For holy and true-
Are the words that Christ Jesus has shared with you.

<u>Jehovah God, the Father, speaking to Earth's inhabitants</u>

Listen to My holy voice, dear ones.
Listen to the voice that speaks to His blessed daughters and sons.

For holy, you see-
Are the words that are spoken by Me.

AS THE HOLY SPIRIT AND PRESENCE OF HASHEM, MY HEAVENLY GOD AND FATHER, SPEAK TO ME

BARBARA SPEAKING

BOWING IN THE HOLY PRESENCE-
OF HASHEM, THE HEAVENLY GOD AND FATHER, WHO DWELLS WITHIN MY EARTHLY RESIDENCE.

BOW, O BLESSED HEAD AND SPIRIT OF MINE!
SHOW UNENDING REVERENCE TO GOD, THE FATHER, DURING THIS BLESSED PERIOD OF TIME.

FOR HASHEM, MY HOLY FATHER AND GOD OF DIVINE LOVE-
SPEAKS TO ME FROM SWEET HEAVEN ABOVE.

BARBARA SPEAKING TO HASHEM; ALMIGHTY GOD, THE FATHER

I AM LISTENING, O BLESSED HASHEM, MY HEAVENLY FATHER AND GOD.
I AM LISTENING TO AND RECEIVING YOUR WORDS OF DIVINE LOVE.

FOR YOU DO LOVE DEARLY-
ALL OF THE CHILDREN OF GOD ALMIGHTY.

HOLY, HOLY, HOLY AND TRUE-
ARE THE BLESSED LOVED ONES WHO BELONG TO YOU.

HOLY, HOLY, HOLY AND TRUE-
ARE THE BLESSED SONS AND DAUGHTERS WHO BELIEVE IN WORTHY AND BELOVED YOU!!!

I AM LISTENING, *O BLESSED FATHER OF CHRIST, MY SAVIOR*

BARBARA SPEAKING

I AM LISTENING TO *THE HOLY VOICE AND WORDS OF CHRIST, MY SAVIOR.*

I AM LISTENING TO THE HOLY SPIRIT OF *HE WHO SPEAKS TO ME, HIS TRUSTWORTHY DAUGHTER.*

I AM LISTENING TO THE HOLY VOICE OF *JEHOVAH, MY FATHER AND GOD.*

I AM LISTENING TO *HIS HOLY WORDS OF LOVE.*

FOR *JEHOVAH, THE ALMIGHTY-*
SPEAKS TO LISTENING ME.

BARBARA SPEAKING TO ALMIGHTY GOD, THE FATHER: JEHOVAH

SPEAK, O HEAVENLY FATHER.
SPEAK THE HOLY WORDS THAT ARE MEANT FOR *THE EARS AND SPIRIT OF BARBARA, YOUR PRAISING DAUGHTER.*

I AM LISTENING, O BLESSED ONE.
I AM LISTENING TO THE HOLY WORDS THAT COME FROM *THE MIGHTY THRONE OF GOD, THE FATHER, AND CHRIST JESUS, HIS ONLY BEGOTTEN SON.*

HOLY, HOLY, HOLY-
ARE THE HEAVEN SENT WORDS OF JEHOVAH GOD ALMIGHTY!!!

O BLESSED *YAHWEH, MY LORD AND MY GOD*

BARBARA SPEAKING TO ALMIGHTY GOD, THE FATHER, YAHWEH

O BLESSED ONE-
O HEAVENLY GOD AND FATHER WHO LOVES HIS EARTHLY DAUGHTER AND SON.

O BLESSED YAHWEH, MY GOD AND FATHER-
I PRAISE YOU FOR WATCHING OVER ME, YOUR SENT MESSENGER AND DAUGHTER.

YOU, O BLESSED ONE-
HAVE GIVEN TO US, CHRIST JESUS, YOUR BELOVED AND ONLY BEGOTTEN SON.

I GIVE YOU CONTINUOUS PRAISE-
IN THE MIDST OF THESE PANDEMIC DAYS.

FOR YOUR HOLY PRESENCE ALONE-
REVEALS A LOVE THAT IS FOREVER AND STRONG.

HOLY, HOLY, HOLY AND TRUE-
ARE MY LOVE AND COMMITMENT TO WORTHY YOU.

HOLY, HOLY, HOLY-
IS MY GOD AND FATHER ALMIGHTY!!!

YOU ARE MY LORD AND MY GOD-
YOU ARE THE HEAVENLY ONE WHOM YOUR LOVED ONES WILL FOREVER LOVE.

HOLY, HOLY, HOLY-
IS YAHWEH, THE ALMIGHTY!!!

When *Yahweh* speaks, *my blessed soul rejoices*

Barbara speaking to Almighty God, the Father, Yahweh

Speak, O blessed Father and God.
Speak to *Barbara, your sent messenger of divine love.*

Speak your holy words to me today-
So that I may tell those whom you send me to, *what you have to say.*

Speak to me, *your obedient and faithful one-*
So that I may *reveal your love to your called daughter and son.*

Speak, O holy Yahweh-
Speak to me today.

For *I desire, you see-*
To *receive the holy words that come from Thee.*

Speak, O lovely one!
Speak to me, for the new day has begun.

When *Jehovah* God, the Father, speaks, *my blessed spirit, soul and body tremble with reverence unto Him*

Barbara speaking

When *Jehovah God, my heavenly Father, speaks to me-*
My body, soul and spirit *tremble with respect and reverence for God, the Almighty.*

FOR *MY SOUL AND SPIRIT FEAR, YOU SEE-
THE HOLY PRESENCE OF JEHOVAH, THE ALMIGHTY.*

I TREMBLE IN HIS HOLY SIGHT-
AS *MY BLESSED SPIRIT REJOICES WITH DELIGHT.*

FOR *JEHOVAH GOD, YOU SEE-*
HAS *SPOKEN TO BELIEVING ME.*

*HOLY, HOLY, HOLY-
IS JEHOVAH GOD, THE FOREVER-LIVING FATHER AND GOD ALMIGHTY!!!*

THE ALMIGHTY ONE *HAS ENTERED MY WORLD*

BARBARA SPEAKING TO ALMIGHTY GOD, THE FATHER, *JEHOVAH*

YOU HAVE *ENTERED MY SHELTERED WORLD, O MIGHTY GOD AND FATHER.*
YOU HAVE ENTERED THE ISOLATED WORLD THAT *YOU HAVE ORDERED AND CHOSEN FOR BARBARA, YOUR FAITHFUL AND OBEDIENT DAUGHTER.*

FOR *YOU, O HOLY JEHOVAH GOD-*
HAVE REVEALED TO ME *THE DEPTH AND REALITY OF YOUR UNENDING LOVE.*

FOR *THROUGH THE YEARS-*
YOU HAVE *BROUGHT CLOSURE AND JOY TO MY "UNCHAINED" FEARS.*

I WALK ALL DAY LONG WITH *JEHOVAH GOD, MY HEAVENLY FATHER-*

AS HE REVEALS HIS GRACE AND MERCY TO *ME, HIS SENT MESSENGER AND DAUGHTER.*

O HOLY FATHER ABOVE-
I SING SONGS OF PRAISE, AS I RECEIVE YOUR HEAVEN SENT LOVE.

FOR *HOLY AND TRUE-*
IS THE LOVE THAT *YOUR BELOVED CHILDREN RECEIVE FROM ETERNAL YOU.*

YOU PERMIT ME TO *WALK IN THE MIDST OF YOUR MERCY AND GRACE-*
AS MY BLESSED SPIRIT *CLINGS TO YOUR MARVELOUS FACE.*

FOR *HOLY AND TRUE-*
IS THE GRACE AND MERCY THAT *I RECEIVE FROM ALL POWERFUL YOU.*

I WILL REACH UP TO YOU, *MY GOD AND FATHER-*
AS I DELIVER YOUR HOLY MESSAGES TO *YOUR CHOSEN SON AND DAUGHTER.*

FOR *HOLY AND TRUE-*
ARE MY WORDS THAT *COME FROM BLESSED AND BELOVED YOU.*

HOLY, HOLY, HOLY-
IS MY LIVING FATHER AND GOD, JEHOVAH ALMIGHTY!!!

YOU, O JEHOVAH GOD-
HAVE ENTERED MY EARTHLY WORLD OF LOVE.

A WORLD-
THAT IS GIVEN TO ME, YOUR OBEDIENT AND FAITHFUL LITTLE GIRL.

FOR YOU HAVE GRANTED ME-
A WORLD THAT IS SINLESS AND FREE.

HOLY, HOLY, HOLY-
IS THE WORLD THAT WAS GIVEN TO ME BY JEHOVAH GOD, THE ALMIGHTY!!!

A WORLD THAT IS FREE-
FROM EVERYTHING THAT WOULD BRING HARM TO GOD'S VULNERABLE CHILDREN AND ME.

A WORLD THAT SHELTERS, YOU SEE-
THE SERVANT AND MESSENGER (BARBARA) OF THE FATHER ALMIGHTY.

HOLY, HOLY, HOLY-
IS THE WORLD THAT IS GOVERNED BY JEHOVAH GOD ALMIGHTY!!!

WHEN YAHWEH SPEAKS, MY MIND, BODY AND SOUL LISTEN TO HIM

BARBARA SPEAKING TO ALMIGHTY GOD, THE FATHER, YAHWEH

SPEAK. SPEAK. SPEAK TO ME.
SPEAK TO THE DAUGHTER AND MESSENGER OF *YAHWEH, THE ETERNAL GOD ALMIGHTY.*

SPEAK TO ME, *O GREAT AND HOLY ONE.*
SPEAK TO ME, *AS I SHARE YOUR DIVINE MESSAGES WITH YOUR WORTHY DAUGHTER AND SON.*

FOR *THEY DO DESIRE, MY GOD-*
TO HEAR OF *YOUR HEAVEN SENT WORDS OF LOVE.*

YOU HAVE GIVEN, YOU SEE-
HEAVENLY WORDS THAT ACCOMPANY ME.

YOU HAVE GIVEN-
MANY HEAVEN SENT WORDS *FOR YOUR WELL-LOVED CHILDREN.*

FOR *HOLY AND TRUE-*
ARE THE WORDS THAT DESCEND TO ME FROM YOU.

HOLY, HOLY, HOLY-
IS YAHWEH, THE ALMIGHTY!!!

WEEP, O BENDING KNEES, WEEP! *WEEP IN THE HOLY PRESENCE OF YAHWEH, THE ALMIGHTY FATHER*

BARBARA SPEAKING TO HER BENDING WEAK KNEES

WEEP, O BENDING KNEES, WEEP!
WEEP IN THE HOLY PRESENCE OF *YAHWEH, THE ALMIGHTY GOD AND FATHER, AS YOU BEND WHILE YOU SLEEP.*

GIVE HOMAGE TO YOUR GREAT AND HOLY GOD EVERY DAY—
AS YOU BEND AND PRAY.

BEND, O WEEPING KNEES OF MINE!
BEND IN THE HOLY PRESENCE OF THE MIGHTY YAHWEH,
DURING THIS DEVASTATING PERIOD OF TIME.

FOR ALMIGHTY GOD, THE FATHER—
DESIRES TO SEE THE BENDING KNEES OF BARBARA, HIS
WORTHY SERVANT AND DAUGHTER.

BEND! BEND! BEND!
BEND, O BLESSED KNEES OF MINE, FOR YOU ARE IN THE HOLY
PRESENCE OF YAHWEH, YOUR HEAVENLY GOD, FATHER, AND
EVERLASTING FRIEND!!!

FOR HOLY AND TRUE—
IS THE GOD WHO FORMED BLESSED YOU.

BEND, O BLESSED KNEES, BEND!
SHOW YOUR DEVOTION AND LOVE FOR ALMIGHTY GOD UNTIL
THE VERY END!

FOR HOLY AND TRUE—
IS THE LORD AND GOD OVER YOU.

WHEN YAHWEH, MY HEAVENLY FATHER, WALKS WITH ME

BARBARA SPEAKING TO ALMIGHTY GOD, THE FATHER, YAHWEH

WALK WITH ME TODAY—
O BLESSED AND WELL-LOVED FATHER AND GOD, YAHWEH.

Walk with me *in the midst of the coronavirus-*
as I cling to the realm that houses the righteous.

Walk with *your trusting daughter-*
as I reach out to *Yahweh, my heavenly God and Father.*

Walk with me *throughout the night-*
as *I keep your realm of goodness within my blessed sight.*

For *only you-*
can, and will, *see me, your believing daughter, through.*

O great and holy God and Father of heaven-
cling to me *as I deliver your holy words of love and comfort to your earthly children.*

Cling to me. Cling to me. Cling to me-
in the midst of *this world's tragedy.*

For *holy and real-*
is your presence that I can truly feel.

Within the loving arms of *Hashem, my God and Father*

BARBARA SPEAKING

Within *the arms of eternal life, you see-*
I hold on tightly to *Hashem, the Almighty.*

For *he rules, you see-*
over blessed and chosen me.

HE RULES *MY LIFE, AND MY EXISTENCE-*
AS *I BEHOLD HIS HOLY PRESENCE.*

FOR THE *GREAT AND HOLY HASHEM, YOU SEE-*
TRUSTS FAITHFUL AND OBEDIENT ME.

WITHIN HIS REALM OF DIVINITY-
I HOLD ON TO *THE DIVINE ESSENCE THAT SURROUNDS AND COMFORTS ME.*

FOR *HOLY AND REAL-*
IS *THE PRESENCE OF GOD, THE FATHER, THAT I CAN TRULY FEEL.*

FOR *HASHEM, MY GOD, YOU SEE-*
IS *TRULY VISIBLE TO BELIEVING ME.*

I CAN TRULY SEE-
THE GOD WHO FORMED FROM HIS REALM OF LOVE, *WORTHY AND GRATEFUL ME.*

HOLY, HOLY, HOLY-
IS THE FOREVER-REIGNING GOD ALMIGHTY!!!
HASHEM MOVES, YOU SEE-
WITHIN THE MIDST OF *HIS LOVED ONES AND ME.*

HE MOVES, YOU SEE-
WITHIN THE BODY OF SANCTIFIED ME.

HOLY, HOLY, HOLY-
IS THE LIVING GOD ALMIGHTY!!!

WHEN *HASHEM*, MY GOD AND FATHER, *WALKS WITHIN ME*

BARBARA SPEAKING TO ALMIGHTY GOD, THE FATHER, HASHEM

Walk with me, O Holy Father-
As you take shelter within the body of Barbara, Your sent messenger and daughter.

Walk with me-
As I deliver Your holy words to those whom You deem worthy.

Walk with me-
As I speak to those whom You have placed in front of me, the sent messenger of Hashem, the Almighty.

You are my spiritual heavenly guide-
You, O Holy Hashem, are the love and Father whom I refuse to hide.

Walk with me as I speak-
To those whom Your realm of mercy does seek.

For I truly need, You see-
To feel the holy presence of God Almighty.

Your holy presence alone, You see-
Gives comfort to trusting me.

Holy, Holy, Holy-
Is the indwelling Spirit of Hashem, the Eternal God Almighty!!!

I CAN FEEL *YOUR HOLY PRESENCE WITHIN-*
AS I DELIVER YOUR MESSAGES TO *YOUR WORTHY BELIEVING FRIEND.*

FOR *HOLY AND TRUE-*
ARE *THE FRIENDS WHO ARE CALLED BY LIFE SAVING AND REWARDING YOU.*

BOOK TWO

BEHOLD MY PRESENT TESTAMENT: THE CONTINUANCE OF MY OLD AND NEW TESTAMENTS, *SAYS THE LORD JESUS*

"VOLUME SIXTY ONE"

CHRIST *JESUS, OUR REDEEMING GOD*

BY:

BARBARA ANN MARY MACK

BEGAN: AUGUST 27, 2021

COMPLETED: SEPTEMBER 25, 2021

TABLE OF CONTENTS

DEDICATION 102

ACKNOWLEDGMENT 103

PROLOGUE 104

DEDICATION

TO CHRIST *JESUS,* OUR REDEEMER AND GOD

ACKNOWLEDGMENT

BEHOLD: CHRIST, OUR REDEEMER AND GOD, IS IN OUR BLESSED MIDST TODAY-*ALLELUIA!!!*

PROLOGUE

MY REDEEMING SON SPEAKS, SAYS GOD, THE FATHER

GOD, THE FATHER, SPEAKING

LISTEN, DEAR CHILDREN.
LISTEN TO THE VOICE OF MY ONLY BEGOTTEN SON, FOR *HE SPEAKS TO THOSE FROM EVERY NATION.*

LISTEN TO HIM TODAY-
SO THAT *YOU MAY LEARN OF HIS HOLY LIFE REWARDING WAY.*

LISTEN! LISTEN! LISTEN!
HEAR THE HOLY WORDS OF MY BLESSED SON, *O WORTHY AND WELL-LOVED CHILDREN.*

LISTEN TO HIM TODAY-
LISTEN TO HIM, *AS YOU SEEK HIS HOLY WAY.*

FOR *CHRIST, THE REDEEMING GOD-*
DESIRES THAT YOU GET *A TASTE OF HIS REALM OF UNENDING LOVE.*

HOLY, HOLY, HOLY-
IS THE LOVE OF THE REDEEMER, CHRIST ALMIGHTY!!!

I WAS THE ULTIMATE PRICE, SAYS CHRIST JESUS, THE REDEEMER AND GOD

CHRIST JESUS, THE REDEEMER AND GOD, SPEAKING

I WAS THE PRICE, YOU SEE-
THAT DESCENDED FROM HEAVEN TO RESCUE THEE.

THERE WAS NO OTHER WAY-
THE PRICE WAS WHAT MY DIVINE ESSENCE DID FULFILL AND PAY.

I WAS THE ULTIMATE SACRIFICE, MY CHILDREN.
THERE IS NO OTHER WHO COULD HAVE MADE SUCH A SACRIFICE FOR THE FREEDOM OF EVERY NATION.

FOR MY SACRIFICIAL BLOOD-
EXPRESSED THE FATHER AND MY REALM OF DEVOTION AND LOVE.

FOR HOLY, YOU SEE-
WAS THE BLOOD THAT FLOWED FROM ME.

THE PRICE WAS VERY HIGH-
YES, DEAR ONES! MY EARTHLY FLESH HAD TO DIE.

BUT NOW, YOU SEE-
THAT THE ULTIMATE PRICE DID SET THE FATHER'S CHILDREN FREE.

HOLY, HOLY, HOLY-
IS THE SACRIFICIAL BLOOD OF CHRIST ALMIGHTY!!!

BEHOLD THE REDEEMING GOD, CHRIST JESUS

MY HUMAN FLESH WAS A SACRIFICE, AND THE PRICE THAT I PAID AS A RANSOM FOR MY HEAVENLY FATHER'S LOVED ONES ON EARTH, SAYS CHRIST, THE REDEEMER AND GOD

CHRIST JESUS, THE REDEEMER AND GOD, SPEAKING

MY HUMAN FLESH, YOU SEE-
WAS THE PRICE THAT WAS PAID FOR THE SALVATION OF THE CHILDREN OF GOD ALMIGHTY.

FOR GOD, THE FATHER, AND I-
AGREED THAT THE PRICE WAS VERY HIGH.

BUT MY SACRIFICIAL ACT OF LOVE-
REVEALED THE FATHER'S DIVINE POWER THAT SITS ON HIS MIGHTY THRONE ABOVE.

FOR IN THE FLESH, YOU SEE-
CAME THE REDEEMING CHRIST ALMIGHTY.

OUT OF DIVINE LOVE, YOU SEE-
ALMIGHTY GOD, MY FATHER, HANDED THIS GREAT ASSIGNMENT OF LOVE TO OBEDIENT ME.

HOLY, HOLY, HOLY-
IS THE GENEROSITY OF GOD ALMIGHTY!!!

FOR GOD, THE FATHER, HAS GENEROUSLY-
GIVEN HIS ONLY BEGOTTEN SON; THE FOREVER-LIVING CHRIST ALMIGHTY.

I HAVE SUFFERED AND DIED ON THE CROSS, YOU SEE-
SO THAT *MY SACRIFICIAL ACT OF DIVINE LOVE WOULD SET EVERYONE FREE.*

I WILL DIE NO MORE, YOU SEE-
FOR *MY PHYSICAL DEATH IN THE PAST SETS MY BELIEVING FRIENDS FREE.*

AS *I SIT ON MY HEAVENLY THRONE-*
I WANT MY FAITHFUL ONES TO KNOW THAT *THEY ARE NOT ALONE.*

FOR *CHRIST, YOUR REDEEMER AND GOD OF LOVE-*
WATCHES OVER YOU *FROM HEAVEN ABOVE.*

HOLY, HOLY, HOLY-
IS THE REDEEMER'S THRONE THAT RESTS IN THE HOME OF GOD, THE FATHER, ALMIGHTY!!!

AND MY BLOOD DID FLOW FOR YOU, *SAYS CHRIST JESUS, THE REDEEMER AND GOD*

<u>**CHRIST** *JESUS,* **THE REDEEMER AND GOD, SPEAKING**</u>

IT FLOWED FROM *MY WOUNDED HANDS.*
BY *GOD, THE FATHER'S, HOLY COMMANDS.*

IT FLOWED FROM *MY WOUNDED SIDE-*
TO REVEAL *A LOVE THAT THE FATHER AND I DID NOT HIDE.*

FOR *MY FLOWING BLOOD, YOU SEE-*
WAS SHED, SO THAT *THE WORLD MAY KNOW OF OUR LOVE AND DEVOTION TO WOUNDED HUMANITY.*

FOR *HOLY, YOU SEE-*
IS THE BLOOD THAT FLOWED FROM SACRIFICIAL ME.

HOLY, HOLY, HOLY AND TRUE-
IS THE SACRIFICE THAT MY FATHER AND I MADE FOR YOU.

FOR *HOLY, YOU SEE-*
IS THE LOVE OF GOD ALMIGHTY!!!

FOR, *THE FLOWING BLOOD OF THE WOUNDED CHRIST JESUS-*
WILL LEAD THE SINLESS FAITHFUL ONES *TO THE LAND OF THE RIGHTEOUS.*

HOLY, HOLY, HOLY-
IS THE BLOOD OF CHRIST ALMIGHTY!!!

CHRIST *JESUS*, THE SLAUGHTERED LAMB OF GOD, *HAS COME BACK TO US*

BARBARA SPEAKING TO CHRIST *JESUS,* THE REDEEMING GOD AND SAVIOR

O REDEEMING CHRIST JESUS-
I PRAISE AND BLESS YOU, FOR *YOU HAVE NOT ABANDONED US.*

FOR *YOU HAVE COME BACK, YOU SEE-*
TO RESCUE *THOSE WHO WERE STOLEN AND DECEIVED BY SATAN, YOUR ENEMY.*

YOU DID NOT ABANDON US-
FOR THE BELIEVING ONES CAN *FEEL YOUR HOLY PRESENCE IN THE MIDST OF THE CORONAVIRUS.*

You are faithful, O Holy One.
You are faithful to your vulnerable and sinking daughter and son.

Christ Jesus, my Redeemer and God has come back for me, like He said He would

BARBARA SPEAKING TO CHRIST JESUS, HER REDEEMER AND GOD

O Holy Redeeming One-
O God, the Father's, only begotten Son.

You have kept Your promise, You see-

For you have come back to redeem sinking me.

You have come back to me-
In the midst of the coronavirus tragedy.

For You have promised me in the past, You see-
That You would never abandon me; the servant of God Almighty.

You have exchanged Your precious life for mine-
And my grateful spirit and soul praise You throughout the realm of unending time.

For holy and true-
Is my gratitude to beloved You.

I am truly grateful-
For You, O Living God-are wonderful.

AND HE DID IT *FOR YOU AND ME*

BARBARA SPEAKING OF CHRIST *JESUS'* SACRIFICIAL ACT OF LOVE

CHRIST JESUS, THE SACRIFICED ONE-
GAVE HIS PHYSICAL LIFE FOR *MY WORTHY EARTHLY DAUGHTER AND SON.*

FOR *HE TRULY SUFFERED, YOU SEE-*
FOR *THE ETERNAL SOULS THAT BELONG TO YOU AND ME.*

HE DID IT, YOU SEE-
BECAUSE *HE TRULY LOVES YOU AND ME.*

HOLY, HOLY, HOLY AND TRUE-
IS THE SACRIFICED *GOD WHO DIED ON HIS CROSS OF LOVE FOR ME AND YOU.*

HE HAS REDEEMED *THOSE WHO WILL SIT BY HIS HOLY THRONE ON HIGH*

CHRIST *JESUS,* THE REDEEMING GOD, SPEAKING

I HAVE SET YOU FREE-
SO THAT YOU MAY *SIT BY THE MIGHTY THRONE THAT WAS FORMED FOR ME.*

I HAVE SACRIFICED MY PHYSICAL LIFE FOR YOU-
SO THAT YOU MAY DWELL IN THE HEAVENLY HOME OF *THE GOD AND REDEEMER WHO IS HOLY, ETERNAL AND TRUE.*

FOR *YOU ARE MY CHOSEN ONES-*
YOU ARE *MY FAITHFUL DAUGHTERS AND SONS.*

YOU HAVE *OBEYED AND FOLLOWED MY EVERY COMMAND-*
THEREFORE, O BLESSED ONES, *YOUR ETERNAL SOULS ARE WITHIN MY HOLY HAND.*

YOU ARE MINE-
AND YOU WILL SIT *BY MY HEAVENLY THRONE THROUGHOUT THE REALM OF UNENDING TIME.*

BARBARA SPEAKING

HE HAS *REDEEMED MY LOVED ONES AND ME.*
HE HAS *SET HIS CHOSEN ONES FREE.*

FREE! FREE! FREE!
FREE FROM *THE WORLD OF SIN THAT ONCE CAPTURED MY FAMILY AND ME.*

OH HOW GRAND-
TO SIT COMFORTABLY *IN CHRIST, MY REDEEMER'S, HOLY HAND.*

OH WHAT A DELIGHT-
TO *LIVE IN THE PRESENCE OF MY SAVIOR'S HOLY SIGHT!*

FOR *HOLY AND TRUE-*
IS THE GOD WHO HAS SAVED ME AND YOU.

FOR *HIS SACRIFICIAL BLOOD, YOU SEE-*
REVEALS *HIS UNDYING LOVE FOR FAITHFUL AND BELIEVING YOU AND ME.*

HOLY, HOLY, HOLY-

IS MY REDEEMER AND GOD, CHRIST ALMIGHTY!!!

HE, CHRIST JESUS, THE REDEEMER AND GOD, HAS COME BACK TO SAVE MY SINKING SOUL

BARBARA SPEAKING

IN THE MIDST OF MY CONTINUOUS SIN-
HEAVEN RELEASED CHRIST JESUS, MY REDEEMER AND DIVINE FRIEND.

HEAVEN'S OPEN GATES RELEASED, YOU SEE-
THE HOLY GOD WHO CAME BACK TO RESCUE ME.

HE RESCUED ME FROM THE MANY SINS-
THAT WERE RELEASED FROM A PAINFUL WORLD THAT NEVER ENDS.
FOR THE WORLD OF PAIN AND DESTRUCTION-
HAS CAPTURED MANY OF GOD'S VULNERABLE CHILDREN.

BUT CHRIST, MY REDEEMER, YOU SEE-
REMOVED ME FROM THE SINFUL WORLD THAT CAPTURED MANY OF HIS LOVED ONES AND ME.

HOLY, HOLY, HOLY-
IS THE HEAVEN SENT GOD WHO HAS COME BACK TO SAVE YOU AND ME.

FOR IN THE MIDST OF THESE SIN FILLED DAYS-
I GIVE ALMIGHTY GOD CONTINUOUS PRAISE.

FOR *HIS REALM OF TRUTH, YOU SEE—*
DID *RETURN TO SAVE BLESSED ME.*

HOLY, HOLY, HOLY—
IS THE REALM THAT RELEASED MY SAVIOR AND GOD, THE FOREVER-LIVING CHRIST ALMIGHTY.

BEHOLD: CAN YOU SEE ME, *SAYS CHRIST JESUS, THE REDEEMING GOD?*

CHRIST *JESUS,* THE REDEEMING GOD, SPEAKING

MY CHILDREN—
YES! *YOU FROM EVERY VULNERABLE NATION.*

CAN YOU NOT SEE—
THE HOLY PRESENCE THAT *WALKS IN THE MIDST OF THEE?*

FOR *I AM AMONG YOU TODAY.*
LISTEN TO WHAT *MY HOLY PRESENCE HAS TO SAY.*

LIVE! LIVE! LIVE!
RECEIVE THE LIFE THAT *ONLY YOUR REDEEMER AND GOD CAN GIVE!*

RECEIVE YOUR SAVIOR!
ACCEPT *THE GOOD NEWS THAT IS GIVEN TO MY CALLED SON AND DAUGHTER.*

FOR *I AM IN THE MIDST, YOU SEE—*
OF *THIS WORLD'S DEVASTATION AND TRAGEDY.*

LISTEN TO WHAT *I HAVE TO SAY.*
LISTEN, O VULNERABLE ONES, *AS YOU GO ABOUT YOUR MERRY WAY.*

FOR *THIS WORLD'S TRAGEDY-*
CAN BE *OVER-TURNED BY REDEEMING ME.*

HEED! HEED! HEED!
COME TO ME, *ALL WHO ARE IN NEED.*

FOR *I AM CHRIST, THE REDEEMER-*
I HAVE COME BACK TO *RESCUE MY SINKING SON AND DAUGHTER.*

COME TO US, *O FAITHFUL REDEEMER AND GOD*

BARBARA SPEAKING

COME TO US, *O FAITHFUL REDEEMER AND GOD.*
MAKE KNOWN YOUR HOLY PRESENCE *TO THOSE WHOM YOU LOVE.*

SHOW US YOUR MIGHT-
MAKE KNOWN YOUR HOLY PRESENCE, *AS YOUR VULNERABLE LOVED ONES FIGHT.*

FOR *WE FIGHT, YOU SEE-*
THE CORONAVIRUS THAT HAS *STOLEN MANY SOULS THAT BELONG TO THE CREATOR AND GOD ALMIGHTY.*

COME TO US-
COME, *O BLESSED SAVIOR AND GOD, CHRIST JESUS.*

FOR *WE DESIRE TO SEE-*
THE HOLY GOD WHO HAS COME BACK FOR *HIS LOVED ONES AND ME.*

MAKE KNOWN *YOUR HOLY PRESENCE-*
AS WE *SALUTE AND WORSHIP YOU IN OUR EARTHLY RESIDENCE.*

FOR *YOU ALONE, CHRIST JESUS-*
CAN *SAVE AND RESCUE SINKING US.*

HOLY, HOLY, HOLY-
IS OUR LIVING SAVIOR AND GOD, CHRIST ALMIGHTY!!!

HE HAS RETURNED TO US *IN THE MIDST OF THE INVISIBLE CLOUDS*

BARBARA SPEAKING

I HAVE WITNESSED-
THE RETURN OF *OUR REDEEMING GOD'S HOLINESS.*

FOR *HIS INVISIBILITY-*
WAS *MADE VISIBLE TO CHOSEN ME.*

FOR *I CAN TRULY SEE AND FEEL-*
THE *HOLY PRESENCE THAT IS REAL.*

DEAR BROTHERS AND SISTERS: *CAN YOU NOT SEE-*
THE *VISIBLE PRESENCE OF GOD ALMIGHTY?*

HE NOW MOVES, YOU SEE-
IN THE MIDST OF *NEEDY YOU AND ME.*

FOR *HIS INVISIBILITY-*
DWELLS WITHIN PURIFIED ME.

HE MOVES WITHIN ME-
AS HE LEADS ME TO *THE LOVED ONES WHO ARE CALLED BY GOD ALMIGHTY.*

FOR *HOLY AND TRUE-*
IS THE VISIBLE GOD WHO WALKS IN THE MIDST OF YOU.

O GRACIOUS REDEEMER AND GOD: *I AM TRULY GRATEFUL*

BARBARA SPEAKING TO CHRIST *JESUS,* HER REDEEMING GOD AND SAVIOR

I THANK YOU, *O BLESSED REDEEMER.*
MY TOTAL BEING IS *TRULY GRATEFUL, O BELOVED SAVIOR.*

I THANK YOU-
FOR *YOUR MERCY AND GRACE ARE HOLY AND TRUE.*

I THANK YOU FROM *THE BOTTOM OF MY HEART-*
FOR YOU HAVE TAKEN VERY GOOD CARE OF ME *BEFORE THE NEW DAYS START.*

MY WEAK BODY AND SOUL *DO CLING-*
TO THE HOLY SPIRIT OF *MY REDEEMING KING.*

MY GRATITUDE SOARS, YOU SEE-
IN THE PRESENCE OF *GOD, THE REDEEMING ALMIGHTY.*

HOLY, HOLY, HOLY-
IS MY GRATITUDE TOWARDS CHRIST ALMIGHTY!!!

FOR *HE HAS REDEEMED, YOU SEE-*
THE BLESSED CHILDREN OF GOD ALMIGHTY.

HOLY, HOLY, HOLY-
IS THE LIVING SAVIOR AND GOD; CHRIST ALMIGHTY!!!

WHEN CHRIST, *THE REDEEMING ONE, SPEAKS*

BARBARA SPEAKING

WHEN *CHRIST, THE REDEEMER, SPEAKS-*
I GO OUT AND *MINISTER TO THOSE WHOM HIS HOLY SPIRIT SEEKS.*

WHEN HE GIVES ME *A SPIRITUAL COMMAND-*
I GO TO THOSE WHOSE SOULS AND EVERLASTING SPIRITS *ARE IN HIS REDEEMING HAND.*

FOR *HOLY AND TRUE-*
IS THE HEAVEN SENT ONE WHO *REDEEMS ME AND YOU.*

FOR *SALVATION-*
IS GIVEN TO *THOSE FROM EVERY NATION.*

YES! *CHRIST JESUS-*
DESIRES *THE CALLED ONES TO LIVE RIGHTEOUS.*

FOR *HE SEEKS, YOU SEE-*
THOSE WHO ARE *CALLED TO LIVE EVERLASTING WITH GOD ALMIGHTY.*

HOLY, HOLY, HOLY-
IS THE SAVIOR CALLED CHRIST ALMIGHTY!!!

FOR HE ENTERED EARTH, YOU SEE-
TO SAVE THE CHILDREN WHO BELONG TO THE FOREVER LIVING GOD ALMIGHTY.

WHEN CHRIST, THE REDEEMING GOD SPEAKS TO ME-
I BOW WITH THE SPIRITS AND SOULS WHO HAVE FOLLOWED LIFE REWARDING HE.

FOR CHRIST, OUR SAVIOR-
HAS SENT ME TO DELIVER HIS HOLY WORDS OF LIFE TO HIS BLESSED SON AND DAUGHTER.

HOLY, HOLY, HOLY-
IS THE ETERNAL SAVIOR, CHRIST ALMIGHTY!!!

FOR HIS HOLY WORDS SPEAK TODAY-
ABOUT HIS LIFE SAVING HOLY WAY.

FOLLOW THE REDEEMING GOD-
SO THAT YOU MAY REJOICE WITH US IN SWEET HEAVEN ABOVE.

HOLY, HOLY, HOLY-
IS THE REJOICING REDEEMER; THE ALMIGHTY!!!

CHRIST JESUS HAS REDEEMED MY BLESSED SOUL

BARBARA SPEAKING

I HAVE BEEN REDEEMED, YOU SEE-
BY THE PRECIOUS BLOOD OF THE ONE AND ONLY CHRIST ALMIGHTY.

FOR *HIS SACRIFICIAL BLOOD, YOU SEE-*
SETS ALL OF THE BELIEVING ONES FREE.

I BOW CONTINUOUSLY *IN THE HOLY PRESENCE OF HE-*
I BOW IN THE PRESENCE OF *THE HEAVENLY GOD WHO HAS SACRIFICED HIS PHYSICAL LIFE FOR ME.*

HOLY, HOLY, HOLY-
IS THE REDEEMER; CHRIST ALMIGHTY!!!

FOR *I DO TREASURE, YOU SEE-*
THE MEMORY OF *THE HEAVEN SENT KING WHO DIED ON HIS CROSS OF LOVE FOR ME.*

I WILL GIVE THANKS, YOU SEE-
TO *THE HEAVEN SENT GOD WHO WAS CRUCIFIED FOR ME.*

HOLY, HOLY, HOLY AND TRUE-
IS THE HEAVEN SENT ONE WHO REDEEMED ME AND YOU.

FAITHFUL AND TRUE, *IS THE GOD WHO HAS REDEEMED YOU*

<u>CHRIST *JESUS,* **THE REDEEMING GOD, SPEAKING**</u>

I AM GOD, THE FATHER'S, ONLY BEGOTTEN SON.
I AM CHRIST JESUS, THE REDEEMING ONE.

I AM FAITHFUL, YOU SEE-
TO THOSE WHO *OBEY AND RECOGNIZE ME.*

FOR *I AM CHRIST, THE REDEEMER, GOD, AND KING-*
I AM MY LOVED ONES ON EARTH, EVERYTHING.

I WANT MY LOVED ONES ON EARTH TODAY-
TO KNOW THAT I AM THE ONLY WAY.

I AM YOUR ONLY ROAD AND WAY TO ETERNAL LIFE-
I HAVE BEEN SENT TO EARTH BY GOD, MY FATHER, TO REDEEM EVERY BELIEVING HUSBAND AND WIFE.

I AM FAITHFUL AND TRUE-
I HAVE COME TO RESCUE ALL OF YOU.

I AM HERE TODAY-
SO THAT MY HOLY SPIRIT AND PRESENCE MAY HELP ALL OF YOU FIND MY LIFE REWARDING HOLY WAY.

MY CHILDREN: PLACE YOUR TRUST IN ME ALONE-
AS I WATCH OVER YOU FROM MY MIGHTY THRONE.

CHRIST, THE REDEEMER, HAS COME FOR ME

BARBARA SPEAKING

HE HAS COME FOR ME TODAY.
I WILL SIT STILL, SO THAT MY BLESSED SOUL MAY BEHOLD EVERYTHING THAT HE HAS TO SAY.

FOR HE HAS COME, YOU SEE-
TO SPEAK THE HOLY WORDS THAT HE WANTS TO SHARE WITH ME.

HIS HOLY WORDS REVEAL, YOU SEE-
FUTURE THINGS THAT HE WANTS TO TELL ME.

HIS FUTURE OCCURRENCES, YOU SEE-
PREPARE BLESSED ME.

HE PREPARES ME-
FOR THE THINGS THAT *HE EXPECTS ME TO DELIVER TO THE CHILDREN OF GOD ALMIGHTY.*

FOR *THE FUTURE THINGS-*
COME FROM *CHRIST JESUS, THE ETERNAL KING OF KINGS.*

HE HAS COME, YOU SEE-
TO *ENLIGHTEN OBEDIENT ME.*

FOR *HE DESIRES, YOU SEE-*
THAT *I RECEIVE EVERY WORD THAT COMES FROM REDEEMING HE.*

HOLY, HOLY, HOLY-
ARE THE FUTURE REVELATIONS OF CHRIST ALMIGHTY!!!

AS I SIT AT THE FEET OF CHRIST *JESUS, MY REDEEMER AND GOD*

BARBARA SPEAKING

AS *I SIT AT THE FEET OF CHRIST JESUS, MY REDEEMER AND GOD-*
MY BODY, SOUL AND SPIRIT, CAN *FEEL THE POWER OF HIS UNENDING LOVE.*

FOR *MY BLESSED SPIRIT, YOU SEE-*
IS IN THE HOLY PRESENCE OF *THE FOREVER LIVING REDEEMER AND GOD ALMIGHTY.*

HIS FEET OF LOVE-
DO COMFORT HIS CHILDREN WHO *WITNESS HIS POWER THAT DESCENDS FROM HIS HEAVENLY THRONE ABOVE.*

BARBARA SPEAKING TO THE REDEEMER'S HOLY FEET

O BLESSED FEET-
I WILL CLING TO YOU, *AS YOU LEAD ME TO YOUR LOVED ONES ON EARTH TODAY WHOM YOU WANT ME TO GREET.*

FOR *I WILL GREET, YOU SEE-*
THE LOVED ONES WHO ARE *CALLED BY CHRIST ALMIGHTY.*

BARBARA SPEAKING TO GOD'S CALLED AND CHOSEN ONES

FOR *HOLY AND TRUE-*
IS THE REDEEMER AND GOD WHO SENDS ME TO YOU.

BARBARA SPEAKING TO THE REDEEMER'S HOLY FEET

O BLESSED FEET OF OUR SAVIOR AND GOD-
I WILL *SPEAK TO THOSE WHOM YOU LOVE.*

FOR *MY GRATITUDE-*
WILL BE SHOWN THROUGH THE WORK THAT I DO FOR MY REDEEMER, *IN THE MIDST OF EARTH'S MULTITUDE.*

HOLY, HOLY, HOLY-
ARE *THE FEET OF MY REDEEMER, THE FOREVER-LIVING CHRIST ALMIGHTY.*

CHRIST, THE LIVING REDEEMER AND GOD, *HAS INVITED ME TO SIT BY HIS HOLY SIDE*

BARBARA SPEAKING

HE, CHRIST JESUS, MY REDEEMER AND GOD-
HAS INVITED ME TO SIT BY HIS HOLY SIDE.

HE HAS INVITED ME-
TO BEHOLD THE PRESENCE OF HIS DIVINITY.

HE HAS SHOWN ME-
MANY THINGS THAT ARE HEAVENLY.

AS I SIT IN HIS HOLY PRESENCE-
I CAN FEEL THE GLORY OF HIS HEAVENLY RESIDENCE.

FOR HOLY AND TRUE-
IS THE GLORY THAT HE SHARES WITH ME AND YOU.

AS I SIT AT HIS SIDE-
HE RELEASES A BRILLIANT LIGHT THAT HE CANNOT HIDE.

FOR HIS LIGHT OF LOVE-
COMES FROM HIS MIGHTY HOME ABOVE.

HOLY, HOLY, HOLY-
IS THE BRILLIANT LIGHT OF MY REDEEMING GOD ALMIGHTY!!!

AT HIS HOLY SIDE OF LOVE-
HE SHARES WITH ME THE WONDERS OF SWEET HEAVEN ABOVE.

I WILL CLING, YOU SEE-
TO EVERYTHING THAT HE SHARES WITH ME.

HOLY, HOLY, HOLY-
IS THE REDEEMER AND GOD, THE FOREVER-LIVING CHRIST ALMIGHTY!!!

AS I SEEK YOU, SAYS CHRIST, THE REDEEMING GOD

CHRIST, THE REDEEMING GOD, SPEAKING

AS I SEEK YOU TODAY-
I DESIRE THAT YOU WALK IN THE DIRECTION THAT WILL LEAD YOU TO MY LIFE REWARDING WAY.

FOR I SEEK, YOU SEE-
THOSE WHO ARE CALLED AND CHOSEN BY REDEEMING ME.

I SEEK THOSE WHOM I LOVE.
I SEEK THOSE WHOM I DESIRE TO SHARE MY HOLY THRONE ABOVE.

FOR MY HEAVENLY THRONE, YOU SEE-
HAS PLENTY OF ROOM FOR THOSE WHO DESIRE TO LIVE ETERNALLY WITH ME.

COME, O BELOVED ONES!
SIT AT MY THRONE OF JOY, O BLESSED DAUGHTERS AND SONS!
FOR I DO DESIRE, YOU SEE-
THAT ALL OF MY LOVED ONES SHARE IN MY HEAVENLY GLORY.

HOLY, HOLY, HOLY-
IS THE REDEEMER'S HEAVENLY GLORY!!!

I WILL LISTEN TO MY REDEEMING GOD TODAY

BARBARA SPEAKING TO CHRIST JESUS, HER REDEEMER AND GOD

I AM LISTENING-
TO MY REDEEMING GOD AND HEAVENLY KING.

FOR YOUR HOLY WORDS, O LORD GOD-
REVEAL THE PRESENCE OF YOUR HEAVENLY LOVE.

I AM LISTENING TODAY-
FOR I DESIRE TO TAKE IN EVERYTHING THAT YOUR HOLY SPIRIT HAS TO SAY.

I WILL GRASP YOUR WORDS TODAY, MY GOD-
I WILL HOLD ON TO YOUR WORDS OF LOVE.

FOR YOUR HOLY WORDS TODAY-
WILL LEAD YOUR EARTHLY LOVED ONES TO YOUR HOLY REWARDING WAY.

FOR HOLY AND TRUE-
IS EVERY WORD THAT COMES FROM BLESSED AND BELOVED YOU.

HOLY, HOLY, HOLY-
ARE THE SAYINGS OF CHRIST ALMIGHTY!!!

THE VOICE AND THRONE OF MY REDEEMER AND GOD ARE CALLING ME, SAYS BARBARA

CHRIST, THE REDEEMING GOD, SPEAKING

I AM CALLING ALL OF YOU-
COME, DEAR CHILDREN, FOR I AM HOLY, ETERNAL AND TRUE!

I AM CHRIST JESUS, YOUR REDEEMING GOD AND SAVIOR.
COME TO ME TODAY, AS I CALL MY WORTHY SON AND DAUGHTER.

COME TO YOUR GREAT AND HOLY GOD TODAY.
COME, DEAR CHILDREN, AND FOLLOW MY LIFE GIVEN WAY.

I AM THE REALM OF SWEET ETERNITY-
COME, O BLESSED ONES: COME UNTO ME, AND GOD, THE FATHER ALMIGHTY.

FOR WE HAVE RESCUED, YOU SEE-
THOSE WHO HAVE FOLLOWED THE FOOTSTEPS OF CHRIST, THE REDEEMING GOD ALMIGHTY.

LISTEN FOR MY HOLY VOICE, DEAR ONES.
LISTEN FOR THE HOLY VOICE THAT CALLS OUT TO HIS BELOVED DAUGHTERS AND SONS.

FOR HOLY AND TRUE-
IS THE VOICE AND THRONE THAT CALL OUT TO ALL OF YOU.

SPEAK. SPEAK. SPEAK, O HOLY REDEEMER AND GOD

BARBARA SPEAKING TO CHRIST JESUS, THE REDEEMING GOD

SPEAK. SPEAK. SPEAK-
AND I WILL RECEIVE THE HOLY WORDS THAT I AM COMMISSIONED TO DELIVER TO THOSE WHOM OUR REDEEMER AND GOD DOES SEEK.

SPEAK TO ME, YOUR OBEDIENT SERVANT AND MESSENGER.
SPEAK, O HOLY GOD, TO ME, YOUR FAITHFUL HEAVEN SENT DAUGHTER.

SPEAK YOUR WORDS OF LIFE.
FOR I AM READY TO SHARE THEM WITH *EVERY CALLED HUSBAND AND WIFE.*

SPEAK, O HOLY ONE-
SPEAK THE WORDS THAT *YOU DESIRE THAT I SHARE WITH YOUR BLESSED DAUGHTER AND SON.*

FOR *HOLY AND TRUE-*
ARE THE WORDS THAT ARE SPOKEN BY YOU.

I HAVE SAVED AND RESCUED THOSE WHOM I SOUGHT FROM THE WORLD OF SIN, *SAYS CHRIST JESUS, THE REDEEMER AND GOD*

CHRIST, THE REDEEMER AND GOD SPEAKING

MY CHILDREN-
FROM *THIS WORLD OF SIN.*

I HAVE RESCUED, YOU SEE-
THOSE WHO BELONG TO ME.

I HAVE SET YOU FREE-
AND NOW, *YOU MUST EXHIBIT MY DIVINITY.*

I HAVE RESCUED YOU TODAY-
AND NOW, *I DESIRE THAT YOU FOLLOW MY LIFE SAVING HOLY WAY.*

FOR *HOLY AND TRUE-*
IS THE GOD AND SAVIOR WHO RESCUED YOU.

HOLY AND TRUE-
IS THE REDEEMING GOD WHO HAS BLESSED WORTHY YOU.

I HAVE SET YOU FREE-
FROM THE WORLD THAT DOESN'T RECOGNIZE ME.

FOR HOLY AND TRUE-
IS THE GOD WHO LOVES AND CARES FOR YOU.

HOLY, HOLY, HOLY-
IS THE REDEEMER, CHRIST ALMIGHTY!!!

AND CHRIST, THE REDEEMING GOD, WALKS

CHRIST, THE REDEEMER AND GOD SPEAKING

I AM WALKING IN YOUR BLESSED MIDST, MY CHILDREN.
COME, AND LISTEN!

HEAR THE HOLY WORDS TODAY-
THAT WILL LEAD YOU TO MY REALM OF TRUTH AND HOLY WAY.

RECEIVE MY HEAVEN SENT KNOWLEDGE TODAY-
AS YOU WALK TOWARDS MY HOLY WAY.

FOR I DO WALK, YOU SEE-
IN THE MIDST OF THIS WORLD'S DEVASTATION AND TRAGEDY.

FEEL MY HOLY PRESENCE-
FOR I DO WALK IN THE MIDST OF YOUR EARTHLY RESIDENCE.

I COME IN A FORM, YOU SEE-
THAT IS VISIBLE TO THE CHILDREN AND LOVED ONES OF GOD ALMIGHTY.

RECEIVE ME, DEAR ONES-
FOR TODAY, *I WALK IN THE MIDST OF MY DAUGHTERS AND SONS.*

I WILL TELL THE WORLD ABOUT *CHRIST JESUS, OUR REDEEMER AND HOLY GOD*

BARBARA SPEAKING

TODAY I WILL TELL THE WORLD-
I WILL INFORM EVERY BLESSED BOY AND GIRL.

I WILL TELL ALL ABOUT *CHRIST, OUR REDEEMER-*
I WILL TELL *EVERY LISTENING SON AND DAUGHTER.*

FOR *IT IS TIME, YOU SEE-*
THAT THE WORLD LEARN OF *THE REDEEMER AND GOD, CALLED CHRIST ALMIGHTY.*

FOR *HE IS IN OUR BLESSED MIDST, EVERYONE.*
AND IT HAS BEEN SENT BY HIM, *TO REVEAL THIS GOOD NEWS TO EVERY MAN, WOMAN, DAUGHTER AND SON.*

FOR *CHRIST JESUS, YOU SEE-*
SENT OBEDIENT ME, *TO SHARE THIS GREAT LIFE SAVING NEWS THAT WAS RELEASED BY THE HOLY SPIRIT OF GOD ALMIGHTY.*

THE GOOD NEWS, YOU SEE-
REVEAL THE HOLY PRESENCE OF THE REDEEMING CHRIST ALMIGHTY.

HE SAVES, YOU SEE-
THOSE WHO BELIEVE AND TRUST THE FOREVER-LIVING GOD ALMIGHTY.

HOLY, HOLY, HOLY-
IS THE LIVING GOD ALMIGHTY!!!

I HAVE REDEEMED MY LOVED ONES, SAYS CHRIST JESUS

CHRIST JESUS SPEAKING

I HAVE REDEEMED THOSE WHOM I LOVE-
SO THAT THEY MAY SHARE IN MY HEAVENLY GLORY ABOVE.

FOR MY REDEEMED LOVED ONES, YOU SEE-
HAVE BEEN BLESSED AND SAVED BY ME.

I HAVE SET FREE-
THOSE WHO ARE THE CHILDREN OF GOD ALMIGHTY.

FOR THOSE WHOM I LOVE-
HAVE BEEN SAVED BY MY HOLY DOVE (SPIRIT).

WALK WITH ME, O BLESSED AND BELOVED ONES.
FOR YOU ARE MY CHOSEN DAUGHTERS AND SONS.

WALK WITH CHRIST, YOUR REDEEMER AND GOD-
WALK WITH ME, DEAR ONES, AS I EXPRESS MY DIVINE LOVE.

FOR HOLY AND TRUE-
IS THE HEAVENLY GOD WHO HAS REDEEMED BELOVED YOU.

AND CHRIST, THE REDEEMING GOD, DID SPEAK

CHRIST JESUS SPEAKING TO BARBARA, HIS SENT PROPHETESS

LISTEN! LISTEN! LISTEN!
LISTEN TO THE HOLY WORDS THAT *I DESIRE TO SPEAK TO MY CHILDREN.*

LISTEN, O BLESSED DAUGHTER (BARBARA)!
LISTEN TO THE WORDS THAT *COME FROM ME, YOUR BLESSED REDEEMER, GOD AND FATHER.*

LISTEN TO *EVERY WORD THAT I SPEAK-*
FOR THEY ARE FOR *THOSE WHOM I SEEK.*

LISTEN, DEAR BARBARA!
LISTEN TO THE HOLY WORDS THAT I SHARE TODAY, WITH YOU, MY FAITHFUL AND CHOSEN DAUGHTER.

FOR *MY WORDS, YOU SEE-*
REVEAL *THE TRUTH ABOUT YOUR REDEEMER AND GOD; CHRIST ALMIGHTY.*

LISTEN TO ME, O BLESSED ONE.
RECEIVE THE HOLY *WORDS THAT I DESIRE TO REACH THE MINDS OF MY BELOVED DAUGHTER AND SON.*

FOR *WHEN I SPEAK TO YOU-*
I WANT YOU TO *RECEIVE THE WORDS THAT ARE HOLY AND TRUE.*

DEAR DAUGHTER: *SPEAK FOR ME.*
SPEAK THE HOLY WORDS THAT *COME FROM THE LOVING GOD ALMIGHTY.*

FOR *MY WORDS, YOU SEE-*
WILL BRING MY LOVED ONES TO ME.

YOU, O GREAT REDEEMER AND GOD, *ARE MY EVERYTHING*

BARBARA SPEAKING TO CHRIST, THE REDEEMING GOD

YOU, O GREAT AND HOLY REDEEMING GOD, ARE MY EVERYTHING.
FOR *YOU ARE MY HEAVEN SENT SAVIOR AND KING.*

YOU HAVE *REDEEMED YOUR LOVED ONES AND ME-*
IN THE MIDST OF *THIS WORLD'S TRAGEDY.*

I BOW *IN THE MIDST OF MY GRATITUDE-*
AS I SHARE *YOUR HEAVEN SENT WORDS WITH EARTH'S MULTITUDE.*

FOR *HOLY AND TRUE-*
ARE THE GOOD BLESSINGS THAT *DESCENDED WITH YOU.*

YOU ARE EVERYTHING THAT I NEED-
I WILL DELIVER YOUR FOOD OF LOVE TO *THOSE WHOM YOU DESIRE TO FEED.*

FOR *YOUR HEAVEN SENT WORDS OF LOVE-*
IS *THE FOOD THAT DESCENDS TO YOUR CHILDREN FROM SWEET PARADISE ABOVE.*

HOLY, HOLY, HOLY-
IS THE FOOD THAT DESCENDS FROM MY REDEEMING GOD, CHRIST ALMIGHTY!!!

HOLY, HOLY, HOLY-
IS THE REDEEMING CHRIST ALMIGHTY!!!

AS I WALK WITH MY REDEEMER AND GOD ON EARTH TODAY

BARBARA SPEAKING

HE IS WALKING WITH ME TODAY.
YES! CHRIST JESUS, OUR REDEEMER AND GOD, WALKS WITH ME, AS I LEAD HIS EARTHLY LOVED ONES TO HIS LIFE SAVING WAY.

FOR HE IS IN OUR BLESSED MIDST DEAR ONES.
HE IS WALKING IN THE MIDST OF HIS DAUGHTERS AND SONS.

HE DESIRES, YOU SEE-
THAT ALL OF HIS LOVED ONES LEARN OF LIFE REWARDING CHRIST ALMIGHTY.

HE MOVES WITHIN ME-
AS I DELIVER THE HEAVEN SENT WORD THAT BRING COMFORT TO BLESSED YOU AND ME, THE MESSENGER OF GOD ALMIGHTY.

AS I WALK WITH CHRIST JESUS TODAY-
I BOW IN HIS HOLY PRESENCE AS I SPEAK OF HIS LIFE SAVING HOLY WAY.

I SPEAK OF HIS HEAVENLY GLORY-
AS I SHARE THE BEAUTY AND REALITY OF HIS HOLY UNENDING STORY.

FOR *HOLY AND TRUE-*
IS *THE REDEEMING GOD WHO WALKS IN THE MIDST OF ME AND YOU.*

I HAVE EXCHANGED MY LIFE FOR YOURS, *SAYS CHRIST JESUS, OUR REDEEMER AND GOD*

CHRIST *JESUS,* OUR REDEEMER AND GOD, SPEAKING TO HIS EARTHLY SISTERS AND BROTHERS

AS *THE SACRIFICIAL LAMB OF GOD, OUR FATHER-*
I DID DIE ON THE CROSS OF LOVE *TO HELP MY EARTHLY SISTER AND BROTHER.*

BECAUSE OF *THE ORIGINAL SIN* **(DISOBEDIENCE TO GOD, THE FATHER).**
I HAD TO *EXCHANGE MY HOLY LIFE FOR MY EARTHLY LOVED ONE AND FRIEND.*

FOR *ADAM AND EVE-*
WERE THE *FIRST TO BE DECEIVED.*

THEY WERE *FOOLED BY SATAN-*
WHICH CAUSED SIN TO ENTER THE WORLD OF *THE DISOBEDIENT HUMAN.*

SATAN, *THE FALLEN ANGEL AND DEVIL, YOU SEE-*
TOLD LIES TO EVE, WHICH *PLACED HER IN CAPTIVITY.*

FOR *THEY WERE TOLD BY ALMIGHTY GOD-*
NOT TO EAT FROM *THE TREE OF KNOWLEDGE OF GOOD AND EVIL, WHICH WOULD REMOVE THEM FROM GOD'S REALM OF LOVE.*

BUT SATAN, YOU SEE-
CONVINCED EVE, ADAM'S WIFE, TO DISOBEY GOD ALMIGHTY.

EVEN TODAY-
SATAN TELLS GOD'S CHILDREN LIES, SO THAT THEY WILL NOT FOLLOW CHRIST JESUS' LIFE SAVING WAY.

AS A PAYMENT FOR THE LIVES OF THE SINNING ONES-
GOD, THE FATHER, PERMITTED HIS ONLY BEGOTTEN SON, CHRIST JESUS, TO EXCHANGE HIS DIVINE LIFE FOR THE LIVES OF HIS EARTHLY DAUGHTERS AND SONS.

BECAUSE THE REMEDY WAS SO GREAT, YOU SEE-
ONLY SOMEONE HOLY COULD COMPLETE A SACRIFICE THAT WOULD SET THE SINNERS FREE.

SO ALMIGHTY GOD, THE FATHER, SACRIFICED HIS ONLY BEGOTTEN HOLY SON (CHRIST JESUS)-
TO DIE ON THE CROSS, AND GIVE FREEDOM FROM SIN TO EVERYONE.

FOR EVERYONE WHO FOLLOWS THE TEACHINGS OF CHRIST JESUS, YOU SEE-
WILL SURELY FROM SIN, BE SET FREE.

HOLY, HOLY, HOLY-
IS THE REDEEMING SACRIFICIAL LAMB OF GOD, CALLED CHRIST ALMIGHTY!!!

FOR HE DOES SET FREE-
THOSE WHO DESIRE TO LIVE THROUGHOUT SWEET ETERNITY.

I WILL WAIT FOR CHRIST JESUS: I WILL WAIT FOR MY REDEEMER AND GOD

BARBARA SPEAKING

I WILL WAIT FOR MY REDEEMER.
I WILL WAIT FOR CHRIST, MY SAVIOR.

FOR HE HAS COME, YOU SEE-
HE HAS COME BACK TO RESCUE YOU AND ME.

FOR THERE ARE MANY, YOU SEE-
WHO NEED THE HEAVENLY TOUCH OF THE REDEEMER AND GOD; CHRIST ALMIGHTY.

FOR HE PROMISED, YOU SEE-
TO COME BACK FOR NEEDY YOU AND ME.

I WILL WAIT-
FOR HIS HOLY PRESENCE TO EXIT HEAVEN'S SWEET GATE.

FOR HIS HOLY WORD-
UTTERS THINGS THAT WE HAVE NEVER BEFORE HEARD.

I WILL WAIT AND LISTEN-
FOR OUR REDEEMER AND GOD TO COME TO HIS EARTHLY CHILDREN.

FOR HE PROMISED, YOU SEE-
THAT HE WOULD NEVER ABANDON HIS LOVED ONES AND ME.

HOLY, HOLY, HOLY-
IS THE FAITHFUL REDEEMER AND GOD; CHRIST ALMIGHTY!!!

CHRIST, THE REDEEMER AND GOD, *RESCUED US FROM THE REALM OF EVERLASTING DESTRUCTION*

BARBARA SPEAKING

CHRIST JESUS' PHYSICAL DEATH, YOU SEE-
IS THE PRICE THAT HE HAD TO PAY, *IN ORDER TO SAVE AND FREE YOU AND ME.*

FOR *HIS SACRIFICIAL BODY OF LOVE-*
CAME TO US *FROM SWEET HEAVEN ABOVE.*

HE EXCHANGED, YOU SEE-
HIS HOLY BEING FOR YOU AND ME.

HIS DEATH *WAS THE ONLY PRICE, YOU SEE-*
THAT WOULD *SAVE SINFUL YOU AND ME.*

FOR ALMIGHTY GOD, HIS FATHER, *IN HEAVEN ABOVE-*
GAVE TO HIS EARTHLY CHILDREN, *HIS ONLY BEGOTTEN SON OF LOVE.*

FOR *CHRIST JESUS, YOU SEE-*
WAS *THE SACRIFICED ONE WHO DIED FOR YOU AND ME.*

HOLY, HOLY, HOLY-
IS THE SACRIFICED ONE; CHRIST ALMIGHTY!!!

CLEANSE YOURSELVES TODAY, *SAYS CHRIST, THE REDEEMING GOD*

CHRIST JESUS, THE REDEEMING GOD, SPEAKING

DEAR LOVED ONES OF MINE-
YOU MUST CLEANSE YOUR BODIES AND SOULS DURING THIS CRUCIAL PERIOD OF TIME.

FOR SATAN, YOU SEE-
IS STILL TRYING TO STEAL THE VULNERABLE SOULS THAT ARE CALLED BY ME.

CLEANSE YOURSELVES TODAY-
BY FOLLOWING MY LIFE SAVING HOLY WAY.

THERE ARE NO OTHER WAYS-
THAT CAN PURIFY YOU IN THE MIDST OF THESE PANDEMIC DAYS.

HURRY! HURRY! HURRY!
RUN TO THE REALM THAT IS RULED AND GOVERNED BY GOD ALMIGHTY!!!

FOR DOOM IS IN YOUR MIDST, YOU SEE-
DOOM IS IN THE MIDST OF THOSE WHO DO NOT FOLLOW ME.

FLEE! FLEE! FLEE!
FLEE TO MY REALM, O BLESSED ONES WHO BELONG TO ME!

CHRIST, OUR REDEEMER AND GOD, SPOKE TO ME EARLY ONE MORNING

BARBARA SPEAKING

OUR REDEEMER AND GOD, SPOKE TO ME EARLY ONE MORNING.

HE TOLD ME TO WRITE DOWN EVERYTHING.

AS HE SPOKE TO ME-
HIS EVERY SPOKEN WORD WAS INAUDIBLE, YOU SEE.

HIS WORDS WERE PLACED WITHIN MY MIND-
AS HE REVEALED EVERYTHING TO ME ONE AT A TIME.

HE SPOKE, AND I DID LISTEN.
HE REVEALED THE THINGS THAT HE WANTED ME TO REPEAT TO HIS EARTHLY CHILDREN.

HE WANTS US TO KNOW, YOU SEE-
THE THINGS THAT ARE UNHOLY IN THE EYES OF GOD ALMIGHTY.

HE SPOKE OF THE PAIN THAT HE DOES EXPERIENCE-
AS THE SINNING ONES DISRESPECT HIM IN HIS HOLY PRESENCE.

HE SAID THAT HE DOES LISTEN-
TO THE DISRESPECT THAT COMES FROM THE MOUTHS OF HIS UNHOLY AND SINNING CHILDREN.

CHRIST, THE REDEEMER-
REVEALED MANY UNPLEASANT THINGS TO ME, HIS SENT MESSENGER.

HE REVEALED TO ME-
THE FINAL DESTINATION OF THOSE WHO DISRESPECT GOD ALMIGHTY.

OH HOW SAD, YOU SEE-
THE DESTINATION OF THOSE WHO ARE FOUND UNWORTHY.

FOR *HOLY AND TRUE-*
IS THE REDEEMING GOD WHO WILL FINALLY JUDGE ME AND YOU.

HOLY, HOLY, HOLY-
IS THE FINAL JUDGEMENT OF CHRIST ALMIGHTY!!!

MY OTHER PUBLISHED BOOKS

1. WORDS OF INSPIRATION
2. FATHER, ARE YOU CALLING ME? *(CHILDREN'S BOOK)*
3. DAUGHTER OF COURAGE
4. A HOUSE DIVIDED CANNOT STAND
5. TASTE AND SEE THE GOODNESS OF THE LORD
6. HUMILITY- THE COST OF DISCIPLESHIP
7. WILL YOU BE MY BRIDE FIRST?
8. ODE TO MY BELOVED
9. FATHER, THEY KNOW NOT WHAT THEY DO
10. IN MY FATHER'S HOUSE (*CHILDREN'S BOOK*)
11. IN MY GARDEN (*CHILDREN'S BOOK*)
12. THE BATTLE IS OVER
13. THE GOSPEL ACCORDING TO THE LAMB'S BRIDE
14. THE PRESENT TESTAMENT
15. THE PRESENT TESTAMENT VOL. 2
16. THE PRESENT TESTAMENT VOL. 3
17. THE PRESENT TESTAMENT VOL. 4
18. THE PRESENT TESTAMENT VOL. 5
19. THE PRESENT TESTAMENT VOL. 6

20. THE PRESENT TESTAMENT VOL. 7
21. THE PRESENT TESTAMENT VOL. 8
22. THE PRESENT TESTAMENT VOL. 9
23. THE PRESENT TESTAMENT VOL. 10
24. THE PRESENT TESTAMENT VOL. 11
25. THE PRESENT TESTAMENT VOL. 12
26. THE PRESENT TESTAMENT VOL. 13
27. THE PRESENT TESTAMENT VOL. 14
28. THE PRESENT TESTAMENT VOL. 15
29. THE PRESENT TESTAMENT VOL. 16
30. THE PRESENT TESTAMENT VOL. 17
31. BEHOLD THE PRESENT TESTAMENT "VOLUMES 18, 19, 20, 21, 22 AND 23"
32. BEHOLD MY PRESENT TESTAMENT "VOLUMES 24 AND 25"
33. BEHOLD MY PRESENT TESTAMENT "VOLUMES 26, 27, 28 AND 29"
34. BEHOLD MY PRESENT TESTAMENT "VOLUMES 30, 31 AND 32"
35. BEHOLD MY PRESENT TESTAMENT "VOLUMES 33 AND 34"
36. BEHOLD MY PRESENT TESTAMENT "VOLUMES 35, 36 AND 37"
37. BEHOLD MY PRESENT TESTAMENT "VOLUMES 38 & 39"
38. BEHOLD MY PRESENT TESTAMENT "VOLUMES 40 & 41"

39. BEHOLD MY PRESENT TESTAMENT "VOLUMES 42 & 43"
40. BEHOLD MY PRESENT TESTAMENT "VOLUMES 44 & 45"
41. BEHOLD MY PRESENT TESTAMENT "VOLUME 46"
42. BEHOLD MY PRESENT TESTAMENT "VOLUMES 47 & 48"
43. BEHOLD MY PRESENT TESTAMENT "VOLUMES 49 & 50"
44. BEHOLD MY PRESENT TESTAMENT "VOLUME 51"
45. LET THERE BE *LOVE—CHILDREN'S BOOK*
46. BEHOLD MY PRESENT TESTAMENT: "*A NEW BIRTH* - VOLUMES 52-56"
47. BEHOLD MY PRESENT TESTAMENT, VOLUME 57 *JESUS: KING OF PEACE*
48. BEHOLD MY PRESENT TESTAMENT, VOLUME 58 AND 59 "TO BE SURROUNDED BY ALMIGHTY GOD, THE BLESSED AND HOLY TRINITY"

CPSIA information can be obtained
at www.ICGtesting.com
Printed in the USA
LVHW071917101121
702990LV00020B/316